THE BUILDING BLOCKS OF LIFE

EXAMINING BIOCHEMICAL REACTIONS

Edited by **Louise Eaton** and **Kara Rogers**

Britannica®
Educational Publishing

IN ASSOCIATION WITH

ROSEN
EDUCATIONAL SERVICES

Published in 2018 by Britannica Educational Publishing (a trademark of Encyclopædia Britannica, Inc.) in association with The Rosen Publishing Group, Inc. 29 East 21st Street, New York, NY 10010

Distributed exclusively by Rosen Publishing.
To see additional Britannica Educational Publishing titles, go to rosenpublishing.com.

Britannica Educational Publishing
J.E. Luebering: Executive Director, Core Editorial
Andrea R. Field: Managing Editor, Compton's by Britannica

Rosen Publishing
Meredith Day: Editor
Nelson Sá: Art Director
Brian Garvey: Designer
Ellina Litmanovich: Book Layout
Cindy Reiman: Photography Manager
Nicole DiMella: Photo Researcher

Library of Congress Cataloging-in-Publication Data

Names: Eaton, Louise, editor. | Rogers, Kara, editor.
Title: Examining biochemical reactions / edited by Louise Eaton and Kara Rogers.
Description: New York : Britannica Educational Publishing in Association with Rosen Educational Services, 2018. | Series: The building blocks of life | Audience: Grades 9–12. | Includes bibliographical references and index.
Identifiers: LCCN 2017011651 | ISBN 9781538300060 (library bound : alk. paper)
Subjects: LCSH: Biochemistry—Juvenile literature. | Bioorganic chemistry—Juvenile literature. | Metabolism—Juvenile literature.
Classification: LCC QP514.2 .E93 2018 | DDC 572—dc23
LC record available at https://lccn.loc.gov/2017011651

Manufactured in Malaysia

Photo credits: Cover, p. 1 (DNA) Jezperklauzen/iStock/Thinkstock; cover. p. 1 (molecule) molekuul_be/Shutterstock.com; p. 10 De Agostini Picture Library/Getty Images; p. 13 BBC Hulton Picture Library; p. 23 Ulrich Baumgarten/Getty Images; p. 38 Shaiith/Shutterstock.com; p. 40 P. Rona, Photographer/OAR/National Undersea Research Program (NURP)/NOAA; p. 102 ullstein bild/Getty Images; p. 236 saasemen/Shutterstock.com; p. 248 digidreamgrafix//Shutterstock.com; p. 289 NaturePL/SuperStock; p. 291 Ylem; p. 301 HTU/Shutterstock.com. All other illustrations, diagrams, and chemical equations Encyclopædia Britannica, Inc.

CONTENTS

CHAPTER 6

CHAPTER 7

INTRODUCTION

The study of the chemical substances and processes that occur in plants, animals, and microorganisms has long formed a vital area of science. Biochemical reactions constitute the driving force behind the constant change of organisms, from changes that occur during development to changes that mark the evolution of life. The field of biochemistry deals with the chemistry of life, and as such it draws on the techniques of analytical, organic, and physical chemistry, as well as those of physiologists concerned with the molecular basis of vital processes. All chemical changes within the organism—either the degradation of substances (generally to gain necessary energy) or the buildup of complex molecules necessary for life processes—are collectively described by the term *metabolism*. These chemical changes depend on the action of organic catalysts known as enzymes, and enzymes, in turn, depend for their existence on the genetic apparatus of the cell. It is not surprising, therefore, that biochemistry enters into the investigation of chemical changes in disease, drug action, and other aspects of medicine, as well as in nutrition, genetics, and agriculture.

The term *biochemistry* is synonymous with two somewhat older terms: *physiological chemistry* and *biological chemistry.* Those aspects of biochemistry that deal with the chemistry and function of very large molecules (e.g., proteins and nucleic acids) are often grouped under the term *molecular biology.* The field of biochemistry emerged as an official area of science around 1900. Its origins, however, can be traced back much further. In fact, its early history is part of the early history of both physiology and chemistry.

The particularly significant past events in biochemistry have been concerned with placing biological phenomena on firm chemical foundations. Before chemistry could contribute adequately to medicine and agriculture, however, it had to free itself from immediate practical demands in order to become a pure science. This happened in the period from about 1650 to 1780, starting with the work of Robert Boyle and culminating in that of Antoine Laurent Lavoisier, the father of modern chemistry. Boyle questioned the basis of the chemical theory of his day and taught that the proper object of chemistry was to determine the composition of substances. His contemporary John Mayow observed the fundamental analogy between the respiration of an animal and the burning, or oxidation, of organic matter in air. Then, when Lavoisier carried out his fundamental studies on chemical oxidation, grasping the true nature of the process, he also showed, quantitatively, the similarity between

This engraving depicts Justus von Liebig's laboratory at the University of Giessen in the 1840s.

chemical oxidation and the respiratory process. Photosynthesis was another biological phenomenon that occupied the attention of the chemists of the late 18th century. The demonstration, through the combined work of Joseph Priestley, Jan Ingenhousz, and Jean Senebier, that photosynthesis is essentially the reverse of respiration was a milestone in the development of biochemical thought.

In spite of these early fundamental discoveries, rapid progress in biochemistry had to wait upon the development of structural organic chemistry, one of the great achievements of 19th-century science. A living organism contains many thousands of different chemical compounds. The elucidation of the chemical transformations undergone by these compounds within the living cell is a central problem of biochemistry. Clearly, the determination of the molecular structure of the organic substances present in living cells had to precede the study of the cellular mechanisms, whereby these substances are synthesized and degraded.

There are few sharp boundaries in science, and the boundaries between organic and physical chemistry, on the one hand, and biochemistry, on the other, have always shown much overlap. Biochemistry has borrowed the methods and theories of organic and physical chemistry and applied them to physiological problems. Progress in this path was at first impeded by a stubborn misconception in scientific thinking—the error of supposing that the transformations undergone by matter in the living organism were not subject to the chemical and physical laws that applied to inanimate substances and that consequently these "vital" phenomena could not be described in ordinary chemical or physical terms. Such an attitude was taken by the vitalists, who maintained that natural products formed by living organisms could never be synthesized by ordinary chemical means. The first laboratory synthesis of an organic compound, urea, by Friedrich Wöhler in 1828, was a blow to the vitalists but not a decisive one. They retreated to new lines of defense, arguing that urea was only an excretory substance—a product of breakdown and not of synthesis. The success of the organic chemists in synthesizing many natural products forced further retreats of the vitalists. It is axiomatic in modern biochemistry that the chemical laws that apply to inanimate materials are equally valid within the living cell.

At the same time that progress was being impeded by a misplaced kind of reverence for living phenomena, the practical needs of humans operated to spur the progress of the new science. As organic and physical chemistry erected an imposing body of theory in the 19th century, the needs of the physician, the pharmacist, and the agriculturalist provided an ever-present stimulus for the application of the new discoveries of chemistry to various urgent practical problems.

The work of two outstanding figures of the 19th century, Justus von Liebig and Louis Pasteur,

Dutch-born British physician and scientist Jan Ingenhousz is best known for his discovery of the process of photosynthesis.

emphasized the significance of the application of chemistry to the study of biology. Liebig studied chemistry in Paris and carried back to Germany the inspiration gained by contact with the former students and colleagues of Lavoisier. He established at Giessen a great teaching and research laboratory, one of the first of its kind, which drew students from all over Europe.

Besides putting the study of organic chemistry on a firm basis, Liebig engaged in extensive literary activity, attracting the attention of all scientists to organic chemistry and popularizing it for the layman as well. His classic works, published in the 1840s, had a profound influence on contemporary thought. Liebig described the great chemical cycles in nature. He pointed out that animals would disappear from the face of Earth if it were not for the photosynthesizing plants, since animals require for their nutrition the complex organic compounds that can be synthesized only by plants. The animal excretions and the animal body after death are also converted by a process of decay to simple products that can be re-utilized only by plants.

In contrast with animals, green plants require for their growth only carbon dioxide, water, mineral salts, and sunlight. The minerals must be obtained from the soil, and the fertility of the soil depends on its ability to furnish the plants with these essential nutrients. But the soil is depleted of these materials by the removal of successive crops; hence the need for fertilizers. Liebig pointed out that chemical analysis of plants could serve as a guide to the substances that should be present in fertilizers. Agricultural chemistry as an applied science was thus born.

In his analysis of fermentation, putrefaction, and infectious disease, Liebig was less fortunate. He admitted the similarity of these phenomena but refused to admit that living organisms might function as the causative agents. It remained for Pasteur to clarify that matter. In the 1860s Pasteur proved that various yeasts and bacteria were responsible for "ferments," substances that caused fermentation and, in some cases, disease. He also demonstrated the usefulness of chemical methods in studying these tiny organisms and was the founder of what came to be called bacteriology.

Later, in 1877, Pasteur's ferments were designated as enzymes, and, in 1897, German chemist Eduard Buchner clearly showed that fermentation could occur in a press juice of yeast, devoid of living cells. Thus a life process of cells was reduced by analysis to a nonliving system of enzymes. The chemical nature of enzymes remained obscure until 1926, when the first pure crystalline enzyme (urease) was isolated. This enzyme and many others subsequently isolated proved to be proteins, which had already been recognized as high-molecular weight chains of subunits called amino acids.

The mystery of how minute amounts of dietary substances known as the vitamins prevent diseases such as beriberi, scurvy, and pellagra became clear in 1935, when riboflavin (vitamin B_2) was found to be an integral part of an enzyme. Subsequent work has substantiated the concept that many vitamins are essential in the chemical reactions of the cell by virtue of their role in enzymes.

In 1929 the substance adenosine triphosphate (ATP) was isolated from muscle. Subsequent work demonstrated that the production of ATP was associated with respiratory (oxidative) processes in the cell. In 1940 Fritz Albert Lipmann proposed that ATP is the common form of energy exchange in many cells, a concept now thoroughly documented. ATP has been shown also to be a primary energy source for muscular contraction.

The use of radioactive isotopes of chemical elements to trace the pathway of substances in the animal body was initiated in 1935 by two U.S. chemists, Rudolf Schoenheimer and David Rittenberg. That technique provided one of the single most important tools for investigating the complex chemical changes that occur in life processes. At about the same time, other workers localized the sites of metabolic reactions by ingenious technical advances in the studies of organs, tissue slices, cell mixtures, individual cells, and, finally, individual cell constituents, such as nuclei, mitochondria, ribosomes, lysosomes, and membranes.

In 1869 a substance was isolated from the nuclei of pus cells and was called nucleic acid, which later proved to be deoxyribonucleic acid (DNA), but it was not until 1944 that the significance of DNA as genetic material was revealed, when bacterial DNA was shown to change the genetic matter of other bacterial cells. Within a decade of that discovery, the double helix structure of DNA was proposed by biochemists James D. Watson and Francis Crick, providing a firm basis for understanding how DNA is involved in cell division and in maintaining genetic characteristics. Advances have continued since that time, with such landmark events as the first chemical synthesis of a protein, the detailed mapping of the arrangement of atoms in some enzymes, and the elucidation of intricate mechanisms of metabolic regulation, including the molecular action of hormones.

CHAPTER

1

CHEMICAL REACTIONS

A chemical reaction is a process in which one or more substances are converted to one or more different substances. In the reaction, the atoms of the starting substances are rearranged, forming new substances that have different properties. The number of atoms and the amount of mass are the same before and after the reaction takes place; thus mass is conserved. The substances in a chemical reaction may be chemical elements, molecules, or compounds. The substances present at the start of a chemical reaction are called the reactants; the substances formed by the reaction are called the products.

Chemical reactions are a part of technology, of culture, and of life itself. Burning fuels, smelting iron, and baking bread are just some of the human activities incorporating chemical reactions. Chemical reactions abound in the natural world, changing the composition of matter within Earth, on its surface, and in the atmosphere, and driving a vast array of processes in living systems.

CELL CHEMISTRY

A description of life at the molecular level includes a description of all the complexly interrelated chemical changes that occur within the cell—i.e., the processes known as intermediary metabolism. The processes of growth, reproduction, and heredity, also subjects of the biochemist's curiosity, are intimately related to intermediary metabolism and cannot be understood independently of it. The properties and capacities exhibited by a complex multicellular organism can be reduced to the properties of the individual cells of that organism, and the behaviour of each individual cell can be understood in terms of its chemical structure and the chemical changes occurring within that cell.

CHEMICAL COMPOSITION OF LIVING MATTER

In addition to water and salts or minerals, every living cell also contains a large number of organic compounds, substances composed of carbon combined with varying amounts of hydrogen and usually also of oxygen. Nitrogen, phosphorus, and sulfur are likewise common constituents. In general, the bulk of the organic matter of a cell may be classified as (1) protein, (2) carbohydrate, and (3) fat, or lipid. Nucleic acids and various other organic derivatives are also important constituents. Each class contains a great diversity of individual compounds. Many substances that cannot be classified in any of the above categories also occur, though usually not in large amounts.

Proteins are fundamental to life, not only as structural elements (e.g., collagen) and to provide defense (as antibodies) against invading destructive forces but also because the essential biocatalysts are proteins. The chemistry of proteins is based on the research of the German chemist Emil Fischer, whose work from 1882 demonstrated that proteins are very large molecules, or polymers, built up of about 24 amino acids. Proteins may vary in size from small—insulin with a molecular weight of 5,700 (based on the weight of a hydrogen atom as 1)—to very large—molecules with molecular weights of more than 1,000,000. The first complete amino acid sequence was determined for the insulin molecule in the 1950s. By 1963 the chain of amino acids in the protein enzyme ribonuclease (molecular weight 12,700) had also been determined, aided by the powerful physical techniques of X-ray-diffraction analysis. In the 1960s, Nobel Prize winners John Cowdery Kendrew and Max Ferdinand Perutz, utilizing X-ray studies, constructed detailed atomic models of the proteins hemoglobin and myoglobin (the respiratory pigment in muscle), which were later confirmed by sophisticated chemical studies. The abiding interest of biochemists in the structure of proteins rests on the fact that the arrangement of chemical groups in space yields important clues regarding the biological activity of molecules.

Carbohydrates include such substances as sugars, starch, and cellulose. The second quarter of the 20th century witnessed a striking advance in the knowledge of how living cells handle small molecules, including carbohydrates. The metabolism of carbohydrates became clarified during this period, and elaborate pathways of carbohydrate breakdown and subsequent storage and utilization were gradually outlined in terms of cycles (e.g., the Embden–Meyerhof glycolytic cycle and the Krebs cycle). The involvement of carbohydrates in respiration and muscle contraction was well worked out by the 1950s. Refinements of the schemes continue.

Fats, or lipids, constitute a heterogeneous group of organic chemicals that can be extracted from biological material by nonpolar solvents such as ethanol, ether, and benzene. The classic work concerning the formation of body fat from carbohydrates was accomplished during the early 1850s. Those studies, and later confirmatory evidence, have shown that the conversion of carbohydrate to fat occurs continuously in the body. The liver is the main site of fat metabolism. Fat absorption in the intestine, studied as early as the 1930s, still is under investigation by biochemists. The control of fat absorption is known to depend upon a combination action of secretions of the pancreas and bile salts. Abnormalities of fat metabolism, which result in disorders such as obesity and rare clinical conditions, are the subject of much biochemical research. Equally interesting to biochemists is the association between high levels of fat in the blood and the occurrence of arteriosclerosis ("hardening" of the arteries).

Nucleic acids are large, complex compounds of very high molecular weight present in the cells of all organisms and in viruses. They are of great importance in the synthesis of proteins and in the transmission of hereditary information from one generation to the next. Originally discovered as constituents of cell nuclei (hence their name), it was assumed for many years after their isolation in 1869 that they were found nowhere else. This assumption was not challenged seriously until the 1940s, when it was determined that two kinds of nucleic acid exist: deoxyribonucleic acid (DNA), in the nuclei of all cells and in some viruses, and ribonucleic acid (RNA), in the cytoplasm of all cells and in most viruses.

The profound biological significance of nucleic acids came gradually to light during the 1940s and

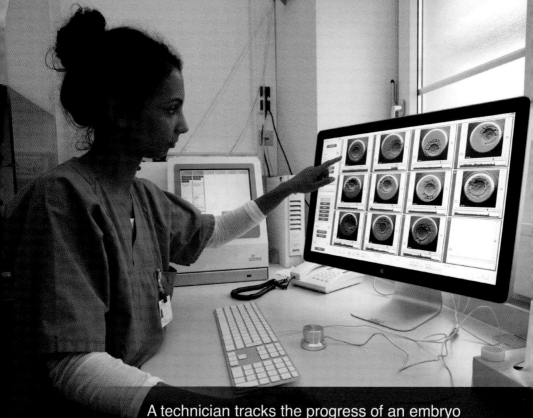

A technician tracks the progress of an embryo fertilized through in vitro fertilization.

1950s. Attention turned to the mechanism by which protein synthesis and genetic transmission was controlled by nucleic acids. During the 1960s, experiments were aimed at refinements of the genetic code. Promising attempts were made during the late 1960s and early 1970s to accomplish duplication of the molecules of nucleic acids outside the cell—i.e., in the laboratory. By the mid-1980s genetic engineering techniques had accomplished, among other things, in vitro fertilization and the recombination of DNA (so-called gene splicing).

NUTRITIONAL COMPONENTS

Biochemists have long been interested in the chemical composition of the food of animals. All animals require organic material in their diet, in addition to water and minerals. This organic matter must be sufficient in quantity to satisfy the caloric, or energy, requirements of the animals. Within certain limits, carbohydrate, fat, and protein may be used interchangeably for this purpose. In addition, however, animals have nutritional requirements for specific organic compounds. Certain essential fatty acids, about 10 different amino acids (the so-called essential amino acids), and vitamins are required by many higher animals. The nutritional requirements of various species are similar but not necessarily identical. For example, whereas humans and the guinea pig require vitamin C, or ascorbic acid, the rat does not.

That plants differ from animals in requiring no preformed organic material was appreciated soon after the plant studies of the late 1700s. The ability of green plants to make all their cellular material from simple substances—carbon dioxide, water, salts, and a source of nitrogen such as ammonia or nitrate—was called photosynthesis. As the name implies, light is required as an energy source, and it is generally furnished by sunlight. The process itself is primarily concerned with the manufacture of carbohydrate, from which fat can be made by animals that eat plant carbohydrates. Protein can also be formed from carbohydrate, provided ammonia is furnished.

In spite of the large apparent differences in nutritional requirements of plants and animals, the patterns of chemical change within the cell are the same. The plant manufactures all the materials it needs, but these materials are essentially similar to those that the animal cell uses and are often handled in the same way once they are formed. Plants could not furnish animals with their nutritional requirements if the cellular constituents in the two forms were not basically similar.

BREAKDOWN OF CHEMICALS

The organic food of animals, including humans, consists in part of large molecules. In the digestive tracts of higher animals, these molecules are hydrolyzed, or broken down, to their component building blocks. Proteins are converted to mixtures of amino acids, and polysaccharides are converted to monosaccharides. In general, all living forms use the same small molecules, but many of the large complex molecules are different in each species. An animal, therefore, cannot use the protein of a plant or of another animal directly but must first break it down to amino acids and then recombine the amino acids into its own characteristic proteins. The hydrolysis of food material is necessary also to convert solid material into soluble substances suitable for absorption. The liquefaction of stomach contents aroused the early interest of observers, long before the birth of modern chemistry, and the hydrolytic enzymes secreted into the digestive tract were among the first enzymes to be studied in detail. Pepsin and trypsin, the proteolytic enzymes of gastric and pancreatic juice, respectively, continue to be investigated. They also have become research tools for modern cell biology and biochemistry. For example, trypsin is used in cell culture to digest the substances formed between adherent cells and the surface of a Petri dish or flask. This frees cells in the culture medium, allowing some to be portioned off for subsequent experiments.

In organisms with digestive tracts, enzymatic action on food generates products that can be absorbed through the walls of the intestines and distributed to the body by blood and lymph. In organisms without digestive tracts, substances must also be absorbed in some way from the environment. In some instances simple diffusion appears to be sufficient to explain the transfer of a substance across a cell membrane. In other cases, however (e.g., in the case of the transfer of glucose from the lumen of the intestine to the blood), transfer occurs against a concentration gradient. That is, the glucose may move from a place of lower concentration to a place of higher concentration.

In the case of the secretion of hydrochloric acid into gastric juice, it has been shown that active secretion is dependent on an adequate oxygen supply (i.e., on the respiratory metabolism of the tissue), and the same holds for absorption of salts by plant roots. The energy released during the tissue oxidation must be harnessed in some way to provide the energy necessary for the absorption or secretion. This harnessing is achieved by a special chemical coupling system. The elucidation of the nature of such coupling systems has formed an important part of biochemical research.

METABOLISM AND HEAT

The cell is the site of a constant, complex, and orderly set of chemical changes collectively called metabolism. Metabolism is associated with a release of heat. The heat released is the same as that obtained if the same chemical change is brought about outside the living organism. This confirms the fact that the laws of thermodynamics apply to living systems just as they apply to the inanimate world. The pattern of chemical change in a living cell, however, is distinctive and different from anything encountered in nonliving systems. This difference does not mean that any chemical laws are invalidated. It instead reflects the extraordinary complexity of the interrelations of cellular reactions.

Hormones, which may be regarded as regulators of metabolism, are investigated at three levels, to determine (1) their physiological effects, (2) their chemical structure, and (3) the chemical mechanisms whereby they operate. The study of the physiological effects of hormones is properly regarded as the province of the physiologist. Such investigations obviously had to precede the more analytical chemical studies. The chemical structures of thyroxine and adrenaline are known. The chemistry of the sex and adrenal hormones, which are steroids, has also been thoroughly investigated. The hormones of the pancreas—insulin and glucagon—and the hormones of the pituitary gland are peptides (i.e., compounds composed of chains of amino acids). The structures of most of these hormones have been determined. The chemical structures of the plant hormones, auxin and gibberellic acid, which act as growth-controlling agents in plants, are also known.

The first and second phases of the hormone problem thus have been well explored. In contrast, there remains much to be understood regarding the third level of hormone investigation—identifying the mechanisms of actions of hormones. Different hormones exert their effects in different ways. Some may act by affecting the permeability of membranes, whereas others appear to control the synthesis of certain enzymes. Some hormones also control the activity of certain genes. For many hormones, however, knowledge of the basic cellular mechanisms through which they exert their various effects is incomplete.

BASIC CONCEPTS OF CHEMICAL REACTIONS

Chemical reactions involve the rupture or rearrangement of the bonds that hold atoms together. The total mass and number of atoms of all reactants equal those of all products, and energy is almost always consumed or liberated. In addition, the speed of reactions varies. In the laboratory, understanding the mechanisms of reactions enables chemists to alter reaction conditions to optimize the rate or the amount of a given product. This type of experimentation provides important insights into conditions that may affect reactions within biological systems. The reversibility of reactions and the presence of competing reactions and intermediate products complicate these studies.

SYNTHESIS

When making a new substance from other substances, chemists say either that they carry out a synthesis or that they synthesize the new material. Reactants are converted to products, and the process is symbolized by a chemical equation. For example, iron (Fe) and sulfur (S) combine to form iron sulfide (FeS).

$$Fe(s) + S(s) \longrightarrow FeS(s)$$

The plus sign indicates that iron reacts with sulfur. The arrow signifies that the reaction "forms" or "yields" iron sulfide, the product. The state of matter of reactants and products is designated with the symbols (s) for solids, (l) for liquids, and (g) for gases.

CONSERVATION OF MATTER

In reactions under normal laboratory conditions, matter is neither created nor destroyed, and elements are not transformed into other elements. Therefore, equations depicting reactions must be balanced—the same number of atoms of each kind must appear on opposite sides of the equation. The balanced equation for the iron-sulfur reaction shows that one iron atom can react with one sulfur atom to give one formula unit of iron sulfide.

Chemists ordinarily work with weighable quantities of elements and compounds. For example, in the iron-sulfur equation the symbol Fe represents 55.845 grams of iron, S represents 32.066 grams of sulfur, and FeS represents 87.911 grams of iron sulfide. Because matter is not created or destroyed in a chemical reaction, the total mass of reactants is the same as the total mass of products. If some other amount of iron is used, say, one-tenth as much (5.585 grams), only one-tenth as much sulfur can be consumed (3.207 grams), and only one-tenth as much iron sulfide is produced (8.791 grams). If 32.066 grams of sulfur were initially present with 5.585 grams of iron, then 28.859 grams of sulfur would be left over when the reaction was complete. The reaction of methane (CH_4, a major component of natural gas) with molecular oxygen (O_2) to produce carbon dioxide (CO_2) and water can be depicted by the chemical equation

$$CH_4(g) + 2O_2(g) \longrightarrow CO_2(g) + 2H_2O(l)$$

Here another feature of chemical equations appears. The number 2 preceding O_2 and H_2O is a stoichiometric factor. (The number 1 preceding CH_4 and CO_2 is implied.) This indicates that one molecule of methane reacts with two molecules of oxygen to produce one molecule of carbon dioxide and two molecules of water. The equation is balanced because the same number of atoms of each element appears on both sides of the equation (here one carbon, four hydrogen, and four oxygen atoms). Analogously with the iron-sulfur example, it can be said that 16 grams of methane and 64 grams of oxygen will produce 44 grams of carbon dioxide and 36 grams of water. That is, 80 grams of reactants will lead to 80 grams of products.

The ratio of reactants and products in a chemical reaction is called chemical stoichiometry. Stoichiometry depends on the fact that matter is conserved in chemical processes, and calculations giving mass relationships are based on the concept of the mole. One mole of any element or compound contains the same number of atoms or molecules, respectively, as one mole of any other element or compound. By international agreement, one mole of the most common isotope of carbon (carbon-12) has a mass of exactly 12 grams (this is called the molar mass) and represents $6.02214179 \times 10^{23}$ atoms (Avogadro's number). One mole of iron contains 55.847 grams; one mole of methane contains 16.043 grams; one mole of molecular oxygen is equivalent to 31.999 grams; and one mole of water is 18.015 grams. Each of these masses represents 6.0221×10^{23} molecules.

ENERGY CONSIDERATIONS

Energy plays a key role in chemical processes. According to the modern view of chemical reactions, bonds between atoms in the reactants must be broken, and the atoms or pieces of molecules are reassembled into products by forming new bonds. Energy is absorbed to break bonds, and energy is evolved as bonds are made. In some reactions the energy required to break bonds is larger than the energy evolved on making new bonds, and the net result is the absorption of energy. Such a reaction is said to be endothermic if the energy is in the form of heat. The opposite of endothermic is exothermic. In an exothermic reaction, energy as heat is evolved. The more general terms *exoergic* (energy evolved) and *endoergic* (energy required) are used when forms of energy other than heat are involved.

A great many common reactions are exothermic. The formation of compounds from the constituent elements is almost always exothermic. Formation of water from molecular hydrogen and oxygen and the formation of a metal oxide such as calcium oxide (CaO) from calcium metal and oxygen gas are examples. Among widely recognizable exothermic reactions is the combustion of fuels (such as the reaction of methane with oxygen mentioned previously).

The formation of slaked lime (calcium hydroxide, $Ca(OH)_2$) when water is added to lime (CaO) is exothermic.

$$CaO(s) + H_2O\ (l) \longrightarrow Ca(OH)_2(s)$$

This reaction occurs when water is added to dry portland cement to make concrete, and heat evolution of energy as heat is evident because the mixture becomes warm.

Not all reactions are exothermic (or exoergic). A few compounds, such as nitric oxide (NO) and hydrazine (N_2H_4), require energy input when they are formed from the elements. The decomposition of limestone ($CaCO_3$) to make lime (CaO) is also an endothermic process—it is necessary to heat limestone to a high temperature for this reaction to occur.

$$CaCO_3(s) \longrightarrow CaO(s) + CO_2(g)$$

The decomposition of water into its elements by the process of electrolysis is another endoergic process. Electrical energy is used rather than heat energy to carry out this reaction.

$$2\,H_2O(g) \longrightarrow 2\,H_2(g) + O_2(g)$$

Generally, evolution of heat in a reaction favours the conversion of reactants to products. However, entropy is important in determining the favourability of a reaction. Entropy is a measure of the number of ways in which energy can be distributed in any system. Entropy accounts for the fact that not all energy available in a process can be manipulated to do work.

A chemical reaction will favour the formation of products if the sum of the changes in entropy for the reaction system and its surroundings is positive. An example is burning wood. Wood has a low entropy. When wood burns, it produces ash as well as the high-entropy substances carbon dioxide gas and water vapour. The entropy of the reacting system increases during combustion. Just as important, the heat energy transferred by the combustion to its surroundings increases the entropy in the surroundings. The total of entropy changes for the substances in the reaction and the surroundings is positive, and the reaction is product-favoured.

When hydrogen and oxygen react to form water, the entropy of the products is less than that of the reactants. Offsetting this decrease in entropy, however, is the increase in entropy of the surroundings owing to the heat transferred to it by the exothermic reaction. Again because of the overall increase in entropy, the combustion of hydrogen is product-favoured.

KINETIC CONSIDERATIONS

Chemical reactions commonly need an initial input of energy to begin the process. Although the combustion of wood, paper, or methane is an exothermic process, a burning match or a spark is needed to initiate this reaction. The energy supplied by a match arises from an exothermic chemical reaction that is itself initiated by the frictional heat generated by rubbing the match on a suitable surface. In some reactions, the energy to initiate a reaction can be provided by light. Numerous reactions in Earth's atmosphere are photochemical, or light-driven, reactions initiated by solar radiation. One example is the transformation of ozone (O_3) into oxygen (O_2) in the troposphere. The absorption of ultraviolet light (hv) from the Sun to initiate this reaction prevents potentially harmful high-energy radiation from reaching Earth's surface.

For a reaction to occur, it is not sufficient that it be energetically product-favoured. The reaction must also occur at an observable rate. Several factors influence reaction rates, including the concentrations of reactants, the temperature, and the presence of catalysts. The concentration affects the rate at which reacting molecules collide, a prerequisite for any reaction. Temperature is influential because reactions occur only if collisions between reactant molecules are sufficiently energetic. The proportion of molecules with sufficient energy to react is related to the temperature. Catalysts affect rates by providing a lower energy pathway by which a reaction can occur. Among common catalysts are precious metal compounds used in automotive exhaust systems that accelerate the breakdown of pollutants such as nitrogen dioxide into harmless nitrogen and oxygen. A wide array of biochemical catalysts are also known, including enzymes and chlorophyll in plants (which facilitates the reaction by which atmospheric carbon dioxide is converted to complex organic molecules such as glucose).

CLASSIFYING CHEMICAL REACTIONS

Chemical reactions are an integral part of life and technology. They determine the appearance and behaviour of organisms and the processes by which foods, plastics, and other products are manufactured. Thus, the ongoing study of reactions is fundamental to both the development of new technologies and the further elucidation of the complicated processes that support living systems.

Knowledge of the basic properties and mechanisms of chemical reactions also influences the way in which chemists group and categorize reactions. Reactions can be broadly classified as syntheses, decompositions, or rearrangements, or they can be additions, eliminations, or substitutions. Examples include oxidation-reduction, polymerization, ionization, combustion (burning), hydrolysis, and acid-base reactions.

Chemists classify reactions in a number of ways: (a) by the type of product, (b) by the types of reactants, (c) by reaction outcome, and (d) by reaction mechanism. Often, a given reaction can be placed in two or even three categories.

CLASSIFICATION BY TYPE OF PRODUCT

The final forms taken by reactants at the end of a chemical reaction are defined as the reaction products. Different reaction pathways result in the formation of different products. Major groups of chemical reactions, categorized on the basis of product type, include gas-forming reactions and precipitation reactions.

GAS-FORMING REACTIONS

Many reactions produce a gas such as carbon dioxide, hydrogen sulfide (H_2S), ammonia (NH_3), or

Bread rises because of the chemical reaction of yeast. One yeast cell can ferment approximately its own weight of glucose per hour.

sulfur dioxide (SO_2). An example of a gas-forming reaction is that which occurs when a metal carbonate such as calcium carbonate ($CaCO_3$, the chief component of limestone, seashells, and marble) is mixed with hydrochloric acid (HCl) to produce carbon dioxide. In the following equation, the symbol (aq) signifies that a compound is in an aqueous, or water, solution.

$$CaCO_3(s) + 2\ HCl(aq) \longrightarrow CaCl_2(aq) + CO_2(g) + H_2O\ (l)$$

Cake-batter rising is caused by a gas-forming reaction between an acid and baking soda, sodium hydrogen carbonate (sodium bicarbonate, $NaHCO_3$). Tartaric acid ($C_4H_6O_6$), an acid found in many foods, is often the acidic reactant.

$$C_4H_6O_6(aq) + NaHCO_3(aq) \longrightarrow NaC_4H_5O_6(aq) + H_2O\ (l) + CO_2(g)$$

In this equation, NaC_4H_5O6 is sodium tartrate. Most baking powders contain both tartaric acid and sodium hydrogen carbonate, which are kept apart by using starch as a filler. When baking powder is mixed into the moist batter, the acid and sodium hydrogen carbonate dissolve slightly, which allows them to come into contact and react. Carbon dioxide is produced, and the batter rises.

Hydrothermal vents, like this "black smoker,"
release fluids that are full of mineral particles.
They were first discovered in 1977.

PRECIPITATION REACTIONS

Formation of an insoluble compound will some-times occur when a solution containing a particu-lar cation (a positively charged ion) is mixed with another solution containing a particular anion (a negatively charged ion). The solid that separates is called a precipitate.

Compounds having anions such as sulfide (S^{2-}), hydroxide (OH^-), carbonate (CO_3^{2-}), and phosphate (PO_4^{3-}) are often insoluble in water. A precipitate will form if a solution containing one of these anions is added to a solution containing a metal cation such as Fe^{2+}, Cu^{2+}, or Al^{3+}.

$$Fe^{2+}(aq) + 2\ OH^-(aq) \longrightarrow Fe(OH)_2(s)$$

$$Al^{3+}(aq) + PO_4^{3-}(aq) \longrightarrow AlPO^4\ (s)$$

Minerals are water-insoluble compounds. Pre-cipitation reactions in nature can account for min-eral formation in many cases, such as with under-sea vents called "black smokers" that form metal sulfides.

CLASSIFICATION BY TYPES OF REACTANTS

Two types of reactions involve transfer of a charged species. Oxidation-reduction reactions occur with

41

DEEP-SEA VENTS

Deep-sea vents, also known as hydrothermal (hot-water) vents, form on the ocean floor when seawater circulates through hot volcanic rocks, often located where new oceanic crust is being formed. Vents also occur on submarine volcanoes. In either case, the hot solution emerging into cold seawater precipitates mineral deposits that are rich in iron, copper, zinc, and other metals. Outflow of those heated waters probably accounts for 20 percent of Earth's heat loss. Exotic biological communities are now known to exist around the vents; these ecosystems are totally independent of energy from the Sun, depending not on photosynthesis but rather on chemosynthesis by sulfur-fixing bacteria. Some of the world's deepest hydrothermal vents occur at depths of roughly 5 km (3.1 miles) in the Cayman Trench, a submarine depression on the floor of the western Caribbean Sea

Deep-sea vents represent one of the most extreme habitats for life on Earth. The animals that thrive there depend on mutualistic symbiosis with bacteria, which synthesize nutrients from inorganic chemicals. The conditions at deep-sea vents are believed to parallel those that were present on early Earth, at the time when life originated, approximately 3.5 billion years ago. Because the geochemical gradients at the vents are capable of producing energy to support life, some scientists have come to believe that the first organisms on Earth appeared in vents. This hypothesis makes use of the known ability of cells to synthesize ATP by harnessing the energy potential generated by chemical gradients and the movement of ions across a membrane.

electron transfer between reagents. In contrast, reactions of acids with bases in water involve proton (H^+) transfer from an acid to a base.

OXIDATION-REDUCTION REACTIONS

Oxidation-reduction (redox) reactions involve the transfer of one or more electrons from a reducing agent to an oxidizing agent. This has the effect of reducing the real or apparent electric charge on an atom in the substance being reduced and of increasing the real or apparent electric charge on an atom in the substance being oxidized. Simple redox reactions include the reactions of an element with oxygen. For example, magnesium burns in oxygen to form magnesium oxide (MgO). The product is an ionic compound, made up of Mg^{2+} and O^{2-} ions. The reaction occurs with each magnesium atom giving up two electrons and being oxidized and each oxygen atom accepting two electrons and being reduced.

Another common redox reaction is one step in the rusting of iron in damp air.

$$2Fe(s) + 2H_2O(l) + O_2(g) \longrightarrow 2Fe(OH)_2(s)$$

Here iron metal is oxidized to iron dihydroxide ($Fe(OH)_2$); elemental oxygen (O_2) is the oxidizing agent.

Redox reactions are the source of the energy of batteries. The electric current generated by a battery arises because electrons are transferred from a reducing agent to an oxidizing agent through the external circuitry. In a common dry cell and in alkaline batteries, two electrons per zinc atom are transferred to the oxidizing agent, thereby converting zinc metal to the Zn^{2+} ion. In dry-cell batteries, which are often used in flashlights, the electrons given up by zinc are taken up by ammonium ions (NH_4^+) present in the battery as ammonium chloride (NH_4Cl). In alkaline batteries, which are used in calculators and watches, the electrons are transferred to a metal oxide such as silver oxide (AgO), which is reduced to silver metal in the process.

Acid-Base Reactions

Acids and bases are important compounds in the natural world, so their chemistry is central to any discussion of chemical reactions. Acids are chemical compounds that show, in water solution, a sharp taste, a corrosive action on metals, and the ability to turn certain blue vegetable dyes red. Bases are

44

NH_3BF_3

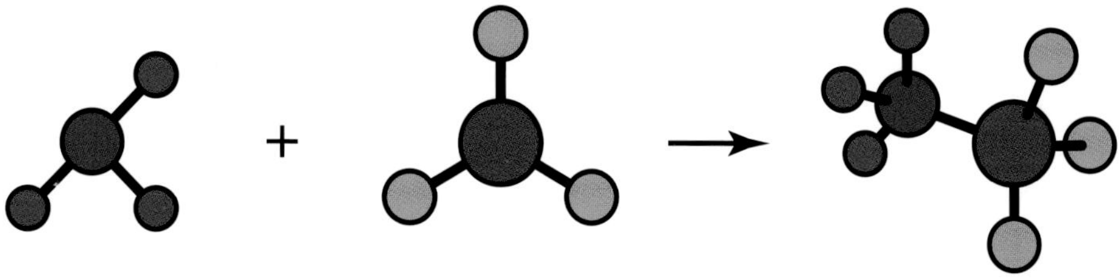

$NH_3{:} + BF_3 \longrightarrow NH_3{-}BF_3$

ammonia + boron trifluoride ⟶ ammonia boron trifluoride

Acid-base reaction with ammonia (NH_3) and boron trifluoride (BF_3) to form ammonia boron trifluoride

chemical compounds that, in solution, are soapy to the touch and turn red vegetable dyes blue. When mixed, acids and bases neutralize one another and produce salts, substances with a salty taste and none of the characteristic properties of either acids or bases.

The imprecise nature of acids and bases has long been a source of intrigue for chemists. The finding that an acid can be displaced from a salt with another acid made it possible to arrange acids in an approximate order of strength. Soon after, however, it was discovered that many of these displacements

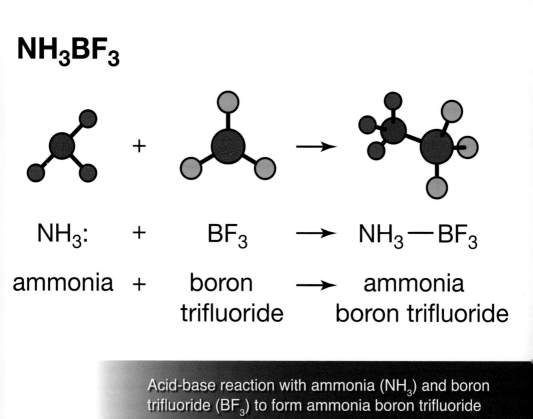

ACID-BASE THEORIES

There are three theories of acids and bases, known as the Arrhenius theory, the Brønsted-Lowry theory, and the Lewis theory.

The Arrhenius theory, named after Swedish physicist Svante August Arrhenius, views an acid as a substance that increases the concentration of the hydronium ion (H_3O^+) in an aqueous solution and a base as a substance that increases the hydroxide ion (OH^-) concentration. Well-known acids include hydrochloric acid (HCl), sulfuric acid (H_2SO_4), nitric acid (HNO_3), and acetic acid (CH_3COOH). Bases includes such common substances as caustic soda (sodium hydroxide, $NaOH$) and slaked lime (calcium hydroxide, $Ca(OH)_2$). Another common base is ammonia (NH_3), which reacts with water to give a basic solution according to the following balanced equation. (The following reaction occurs to a very small extent, and the hydroxide ion concentration is small but measurable.)

$$NH_3(aq) + H_2O(l) \rightarrow NH_4\ (aq) + OH\ (aq)$$

A large number of natural bases are known, including morphine, cocaine, nicotine, and caffeine. Many synthetic drugs are also bases. All of these contain a nitrogen atom bonded to three other groups, and all behave similarly to ammonia in that they can react with water to give a solution containing the hydroxide ion.

Amino acids, a very important class of compounds, are able to function both as acids and as bases. Amino acid molecules contain both acidic ($-COOH$) and basic ($-NH_2$) sites. In an aqueous solution, amino acids exist in both the molecular form and the so-called "zwitterionic" (or hybrid) form, $H_3N + CH_2CO_2^-$. In this structure the nitrogen atom bears a positive charge, and the oxygen atom of the acid group bears a negative charge.

According to the Arrhenius theory, acid-base reactions involve the combination of the hydrogen ion (H^+) and the hydroxide ion to form water. An example is the reaction of aqueous solutions of sodium hydroxide and hydrochloric acid.

$$HCl(aq) + NaOH(aq) \rightarrow NaCl(aq) + H_2O \ (l)$$

Arrhenius's work in immunochemistry, a term that gained currency through his book of that title published in 1907, was an attempt to study toxin-antitoxin reactions, principally diphtheria reactions, using the concepts and methods developed in physical chemistry. Together with Torvald Madsen, director of the State Serum Institute in Copenhagen, he carried out wide-ranging experimental studies of bacterial toxins as well as plant and animal poisons. The technical difficulties were too great, however, for Arrhenius to realize his aim of making immunology an exact science. Instead, it was his spirited attacks on the reigning theory in the field of immunity studies, the side-chain-theory formulated by the German medical

(continued on the next page)

(continued from the previous page)

scientist Paul Ehrlich, that attracted attention. This, however, was of short duration, and Arrhenius gradually abandoned the field.

A somewhat more general acid-base theory, the Brønsted-Lowry theory, named after Danish chemist Johannes Nicolaus Brønsted and English chemist Thomas Martin Lowry, defines an acid as a proton donor and a base as a proton acceptor. In this theory, the reaction of an acid and base is represented as an equilibrium reaction. (In the following equation, the double arrows, $\rightleftharpoons$, indicate that the products can re-form the reactants in a dynamic process.)

$$\text{acid (1)} + \text{base (2)} \rightleftharpoons \text{base (1)} + \text{acid (2)}$$

Acid (1) and base (1) are called a conjugate acid-base pair, as are acid (2) and base (2). The advantage of this theory is its predictive capacity. Whether the equilibrium lies toward the reactants (reactant-favoured) or the products (product-favoured) is determined by the relative strengths of the acids and bases.

The Brønsted-Lowry theory is often closely associated with the solvent water. Dissolving an acid in water to form the hydronium ion and the anion of the acid is an acid-base reaction. Acids are classified as strong or weak, depending on whether the equilibrium favours the reactants or products. Hydrochloric acid, a strong acid, ionizes completely in water to form the hydronium and chlorine (Cl^-) ions in a product-favoured reaction.

A still broader acid and base theory was proposed by American physical chemist Gilbert N. Lewis. In the Lewis theory, bases are defined as electron-pair donors and acids as electron-pair acceptors. Acid-base reactions involve the combination of the Lewis acid and base through sharing of the base's electron pair.

Ammonia is an example of a Lewis base. A pair of electrons located on the nitrogen atom may be used to form a chemical bond to a Lewis acid such as boron trifluoride (BF_3). (In the following equation, the colon represents an electron pair.)

$$H_3N: + BF_3 \rightarrow H_3N- BF_3$$

Ammonia, water, and many other Lewis bases react with metal ions to form a group of species known as coordination compounds. The reaction to form these species is another example of a Lewis acid-base reaction. For example, the light blue colour of a solution of Cu^{2+} ions in water is due to the $[Cu(H_2O)_6]^{2+}$ ion. If ammonia is added to this solution, the water molecules attached to copper are replaced by ammonia molecules, and the beautiful deep blue ion $[Cu(NH_3)_4]^{2+}$ is formed.

can occur in either direction according to experimental conditions. This suggested that acid-base reactions are reversible—that the products of the reaction can interact to regenerate the starting material. It also introduced the concept of equilibrium to acid-base chemistry. This concept states that reversible chemical reactions reach a point of balance, or equilibrium, at which the starting materials and the products are each regenerated by one of the two reactions as rapidly as they are consumed by the other. The significant theoretical interest generated by these factors led to the development of several theories of acid-base behaviour.

BY REACTION OUTCOME

Chemists often classify reactions on the basis of the overall result. Examples of reactions classified in this way include decomposition reactions, substitution, elimination, and addition reactions, and polymerization reactions. As previously noted, many reactions defy simple classification and may fit in several categories.

DECOMPOSITION REACTIONS

Decomposition reactions are processes in which chemical species break up into simpler parts. Usually, decomposition reactions require energy input.

For example, a common method of producing oxygen gas in the laboratory is the decomposition of potassium chlorate ($KClO_3$) by heat.

$$2KClO_3(s) \longrightarrow 2KCl(s) + 3O_2(g)$$

Another decomposition reaction is the production of sodium (Na) and chlorine (Cl_2) by electrolysis of molten sodium chloride (NaCl) at high temperature.

$$2NaCl\ (l) \longrightarrow 2Na\ (l) + Cl_2(g)$$

A decomposition reaction that was very important in the history of chemistry is the decomposition of mercury oxide (HgO) with heat to give mercury metal (Hg) and oxygen gas. This is the reaction used by 18th-century chemists Carl Wilhelm Scheele, Joseph Priestley, and Antoine Laurent Lavoisier in their experiments on oxygen.

$$2HgO(s) \longrightarrow 2Hg\ (l) + O_2(g)$$

SUBSTITUTION, ELIMINATION, AND ADDITION REACTIONS

The terms *substitution*, *elimination*, and *addition* are particularly useful in describing organic reactions. In a substitution reaction, an atom or group of atoms in a molecule is replaced by another atom or group of atoms. For example, methane (CH_4)

reacts with chlorine (Cl_2) to produce chloromethane (CH_3Cl), a compound used as a topical anesthetic. In this reaction, a chlorine atom is substituted for a hydrogen atom.

Substitution reactions are widely used in industrial chemistry. For example, substituting two of the chlorine atoms on chloroform ($CHCl_3$) with fluorine atoms produces chlorodifluoromethane ($CHClF_2$). This product undergoes a further reaction when heated strongly.

$$2CHClF_2(g) \longrightarrow F_2C{=}CF_2(g) + 2HCl(g)$$

This latter reaction is an example of an elimination reaction, a hydrogen atom and a chlorine atom being eliminated from the starting material as hydrochloric acid (HCl). The other product is tetrafluoroethylene, a precursor to the polymer known commercially as Teflon.

Addition reactions are the opposite of elimination reactions. As the name implies, one molecule is added to another. An example is the common industrial preparation of ethanol (CH_3CH_2OH). Historically, this compound was made by fermentation. However, since the early 1970s, it has also been made commercially by the addition of water to ethylene.

$$C_2H_4 + H_2O \longrightarrow CH_3CH_2OH$$

52

Polymerization Reactions

Polymers are high-molecular-weight compounds, fashioned by the aggregation of many smaller molecules called monomers. The plastics that have so changed society and the natural and synthetic fibres used in clothing are polymers. There are two basic ways to form polymers: (a) linking small molecules together, a type of addition reaction, and (b) combining two molecules (of the same or different type) with the elimination of a stable small molecule such as water. This latter type of polymerization combines addition and elimination reactions and is called a condensation reaction.

An example of the first type of reaction is the union of thousands of ethylene molecules that gives polyethylene.

$$nH_2C=CH_2 \longrightarrow [-CH_2CH_2-]_n$$

Other addition polymers include polypropylene (made by polymerizing $H_2C=CHCH_3$), polystyrene (from $H_2C=CHC_6H_5$), and polyvinyl chloride (from $H_2C=CHCl$).

Starch and cellulose are examples of the second type of polymer. These are members of a class of compounds called carbohydrates, substances with formulas that are multiples of the simple formula CH_2O. Both starch and cellulose are polymers of glucose, a sugar with the formula $C_6H_{12}O_6$. In both starch and cellulose, molecules of glucose are joined together with concomitant elimination of a molecule of water for every linkage formed.

$$nC_6H_{12}O_6 \longrightarrow -[-C_6H_{10}O_5-]_{-n} + nH_2O$$

The synthetic material nylon is another example of this type of polymer. Water and a polymer (nylon-6,6) are formed when an organic acid and an amine (a compound derived from ammonia) combine.

The natural fibres of proteins such as hair, wool, and silk are also polymers that contain the repeating unit (-CHRCONH-), where R is a group of atoms attached to the main polymer. These form by joining amino acids with the elimination of a water molecule for each CONH or peptide linkage formed.

SOLVOLYSIS AND HYDROLYSIS

A solvolysis reaction is one in which the solvent is also a reactant. Solvolysis reactions are generally named after the specific solvent—for example, the term *hydrolysis* when water is involved. If a compound is represented by the formula AB (in which A and B are atoms or groups of atoms) and water is represented by the formula HOH, the hydrolysis reaction may be represented by the reversible chemical reaction

$$AB + HOH \rightleftharpoons AH + BOH.$$

Hydrolysis of an organic compound is illustrated by the reaction of water with esters. Esters have the general formula RCOOR′, R and R′ being combining groups (such as CH_3). The hydrolysis of an ester produces an acid and an alcohol. The equation for the reaction of methyl acetate and water is

$$CH_3COOCH_3(aq) + H_2O(l) \longrightarrow CH_3COOH(aq) + CH_3OH(aq).$$

Hydrolysis reactions play an important role in chemical processes that occur in living organisms. Proteins are hydrolyzed to amino acids, fats to fatty acids and glycerol, and starches and complex sugars to simple sugars. In most instances, the rates of these processes are enhanced by the presence of enzymes, biological catalysts.

Hydrolysis reactions are also important to acid-base behaviour. Anions of weak acids dissolve in water to give basic solutions, as in the hydrolysis of the acetate ion, CH_3COO^-.

$$CH_3COO^-(aq) + H_2O(l) \longrightarrow CH_3COOH(aq) + OH^-(aq)$$

Although this is a reactant-favoured reaction, it occurs to an extent sufficient to cause a solution containing the acetate ion to exhibit basic properties (e.g., turning red litmus paper blue). Hydrolysis reactions account for the basic character of many common substances. Salts of the borate, phosphate, and carbonate ions, for example, give basic solutions that have long been used for cleaning purposes. Many food products also contain basic anions such as tartrate and citrate ions.

BY REACTION MECHANISM

Reaction mechanisms provide details on how atoms are shuffled and reassembled in the formation of products from reactants. Chain and photolysis reactions are named on the basis of the mechanism of the process.

CHAIN REACTIONS

Chain reactions occur in a sequence of steps, in which the product of each step is a reagent for the next. Chain reactions generally involve three distinct processes: an initiation step that begins the reaction, a series of chain-propagation steps, and, eventually, a termination step.

Polymerization reactions are chain reactions, and the formation of Teflon from tetrafluoroethylene is one example. In this reaction, a peroxide (a compound in which two oxygen atoms are joined together by a single covalent bond) may be used as the initiator. Peroxides readily form highly reactive free-radical species (a species with an unpaired electron) that initiate the reaction. There are a number of different ways to terminate the chain, one of which is shown in the following example. (In the following equations, the dots represent unpaired electrons, and R is a generic organic group.)

1. Decomposition of a peroxide to radicals:
   $ROOR \longrightarrow 2\ RO\cdot$

2. Chain initiation: $RO\cdot + F_2C=CF_2 \longrightarrow ROCF_2CF_2\cdot$

3. Chain-propagation steps:

   $ROCF_2CF_2\cdot + F_2C=CF_2 \rightarrow ROCF_2CF_2CF_2CF_2\cdot$ $ROCF_2CF_2CF_2CF_2\cdot + (n-2)\ F_2C=CF_2 \longrightarrow RO-(CF_2CF_2\cdot)_n-$

4. A possible chain-termination step:
   $RO-(CF_2CF_2\cdot)_n- + \cdot OR \longrightarrow RO(CF_2CF_2)_n$

PHOTOLYSIS REACTIONS

Photolysis reactions are initiated or sustained by the absorption of electromagnetic radiation. One example is the decomposition of ozone to oxygen in the atmosphere. Another example is the synthesis of chloromethane from methane and chlorine, which is initiated by light. The overall reaction is

$$CH_4(g) + Cl_2(g) + hv \longrightarrow CH_3Cl(g) + HCl(g),$$

where hv represents light. This reaction, coincidentally, is also a chain reaction. It begins with the endothermic reaction of a chlorine molecule (Cl_2) to give chlorine atoms, a process that occurs under ultraviolet irradiation. When formed, some of the chlorine atoms recombine to form chlorine molecules, but not all do so. If a chlorine atom instead collides with a methane molecule, a two-step chain propagation occurs. The first propagation step produces the methyl radical (CH_3). This free-radical species reacts with a chlorine molecule to give the product and a chlorine atom, which continues the chain reaction for many additional steps. Possible termination steps include combination of two methyl radicals to form ethane (CH_3CH_3) and a combination of methyl and chlorine radicals to give chloromethane.

1. Chain-initiation step: $Cl_2 \rightleftharpoons 2 \cdot Cl$

2. Chain-propagation steps: $CH_4 + \cdot Cl \longrightarrow CH_3 +$ HCl and $CH_3 + Cl_2 \rightarrow CH_3Cl + \cdot$

3. Possible chain-termination steps: $CH_3 + \cdot CH_3 \longrightarrow CH_3CH_3$ and $CH_3 + \cdot Cl \longrightarrow CH_3Cl$

THE STUDY OF BIOCHEMICAL REACTIONS

Biochemists study the many complex and interrelated chemical changes of cells in order to understand how reactions effect life processes. For example, biochemists study the chemical reactions that synthesize proteins and all their precursors, convert food to energy, transmit hereditary characteristics, store and release energy, and catalyze all biochemical reactions. These investigations straddle the biological and physical sciences and use many techniques common in medicine and physiology as well as those of organic, analytical, and physical chemistry. In addition, similar to the other chemical sciences, biochemistry attempts to quantify, or measure, results, often with sophisticated instrumentation.

The earliest approach to a study of the events in a living organism was an analysis of the materials entering an organism (foods, oxygen) and those leaving (excretion products, carbon dioxide). This is still the basis of so-called balance experiments conducted on animals, in which, for example, both foods and excreta are thoroughly analyzed. For this purpose many chemical methods involving specific colour reactions have been developed, requiring spectrum-analyzing instruments (spectrophotometers) for quantitative measurement. Gasometric techniques are those commonly used for measurements of oxygen and carbon dioxide, yielding respiratory quotients (the ratio of carbon dioxide to oxygen).

Somewhat more detail has been gained by determining the quantities of substances entering and leaving a given organ and also by incubating slices of a tissue in a physiological medium outside the body and analyzing the changes that occur in the medium. Because these techniques yield an overall picture of metabolic capacities, it became necessary to disrupt cellular structure (homogenization) and to isolate the individual parts of the cell—nuclei, mitochondria, lysosomes, ribosomes, membranes—and finally the various enzymes and discrete chemical substances of the cell in an attempt to understand the chemistry of life more fully.

CENTRIFUGATION AND ELECTROPHORESIS

An important tool in biochemical research is the centrifuge, which through rapid spinning imposes high centrifugal forces on suspended particles, or even molecules in solution, and causes separations of such matter on the basis of differences in weight. Thus, red cells may be separated from plasma of blood, nuclei from mitochondria in cell homogenates, and one protein from another in complex mixtures. Proteins are separated by ultracentrifugation—very high speed spinning. With appropriate photography of the protein layers as they form in the centrifugal field, it is possible to determine the molecular weights of proteins. Another property of biological molecules that has been exploited for separation and analysis is their electrical charge. Amino acids and proteins possess net positive or negative charges according to the acidity of the solution in which they are dissolved. In an electric field, such molecules adopt different rates of migration toward positively (anode) or negatively (cathode) charged poles and permit separation. Such separations can be effected in solutions or when the proteins saturate a stationary medium such as cellulose (filter paper), starch, or acrylamide gels. By appropriate colour reactions of the proteins and scanning of colour intensities, a number of proteins in a mixture may be measured. Separate proteins may be isolated and identified by electrophoresis, and the purity of a given protein may be determined. (Electrophoresis of human hemoglobin revealed the abnormal hemoglobin in sickle-cell anemia, the first definitive example of a "molecular disease.")

CHROMATOGRAPHY AND ISOTOPES

The different solubilities of substances in aqueous and organic solvents provide another basis for analysis. In its earlier form, a separation was conducted in complex apparatus by partition of substances in

EXAMINING BIOCHEMICAL REACTIONS

various solvents. A simplified form of the same principle evolved as "paper chromatography," in which small amounts of substances could be separated on filter paper and identified by appropriate colour reactions. In contrast to electrophoresis, this method has been applied to a wide variety of biological compounds and has contributed enormously to research in biochemistry.

The general principle has been extended from filter paper strips to columns of other relatively inert media, permitting larger scale separation and identification of closely related biological substances.

Particularly noteworthy has been the separation of amino acids by chromatography in columns of ion-exchange resins, permitting the determination of exact amino acid composition of proteins. Following such determination, other techniques of organic chemistry have been used to elucidate the actual sequence of amino acids in complex proteins. Another technique of column chromatography is based on the relative rates of penetration of molecules into beads of a complex carbohydrate according to size of the molecules. Larger molecules are excluded relative to smaller molecules and emerge first from a column of such beads. This technique not only permits separation of biological substances but also provides estimates of molecular weights.

Perhaps the single most important technique in unravelling the complexities of metabolism has been the use of isotopes (heavy or radioactive elements) in labelling biological compounds and "tracing" their fate in metabolism. Measurement of the isotope-labelled compounds has required considerable technology in mass spectroscopy and radioactive detection devices. A variety of other physical techniques, such as nuclear magnetic resonance, electron spin spectroscopy, circular dichroism, and X-ray crystallography, have become prominent tools in revealing the relation of chemical structure to biological function.

CHAPTER
2

CELLULAR CHEMICAL REACTIONS

L iving organisms can extract energy from their environments and use it to carry out activities such as movement, growth and development, and reproduction. These processes—energy extraction and the utilization of this energy to synthesize and assemble cellular components—form the basis of metabolism. The term *intermediary metabolism* refers to the vast web of interconnected chemical reactions by which all the cell's constituents, many rarely found outside it, are created and destroyed. Anabolic reactions use energy to build complex molecules from simpler organic compounds (e.g., proteins from amino acids, carbohydrates from sugars, fats from fatty acids and glycerol), whereas catabolic reactions break complex molecules down into simpler ones, releasing chemical energy.

For most organisms, energy comes ultimately from the Sun. Plants and other organisms that contain the pigment chlorophyll obtain energy by photosynthesis and store it in organic compounds. Other organisms, including humans and nearly all other animals, obtain energy by consuming plants and other photosynthetic organisms. In bacteria that inhabit certain environments, the energy comes from chemical reactions instead. For example, the bacteria of deep-sea vents synthesize their nutrients from inorganic substances in a process known as chemoautotrophy. Within all cells, energy is transferred in the form of adenosine triphosphate (ATP), and whereas anabolic reactions consume energy, catabolic reactions generate it. In addition, every chemical reaction of metabolism, which culminates in the generation of ATP, is mediated by a specific enzyme.

COMMON STEPS IN CELLULAR CHEMICAL REACTIONS

At the cellular level of organization, the main chemical processes of all living matter are similar, if not identical. This is true for animals, plants, fungi, or bacteria. Where variations occur (such as in the secretion of antibodies by some molds), the variant processes are but variations on common themes. Thus, all living matter is made up of large molecules called proteins, which provide support and coordinated movement and serve in the storage and transport of small molecules. Certain proteins also function as catalysts, enabling chemical reactions to take place rapidly and specifically under mild temperature, relatively low concentration, and neutral conditions (i.e., neither acidic nor basic). Proteins are assembled from some 20 amino acids, and, just as the 26 letters of the alphabet can be assembled in specific ways to form words of various lengths and meanings, so may tens or even hundreds of the 20 amino-acid "letters" be joined to form specific proteins. Moreover, those portions of protein molecules involved in performing similar functions in different organisms often comprise the same sequences of amino acids.

There is the same unity among cells of all types in the manner in which living organisms preserve their individuality and transmit it to their offspring. For example, hereditary information is encoded in a specific sequence of bases that make up the DNA molecule in the nucleus of each cell. Only four bases are used in synthesizing DNA: adenine, guanine, cytosine, and thymine. Just as the Morse Code consists of three simple signals—a dash, a dot, and a space—the precise arrangement of which suffices to convey coded messages, so the precise arrangement of the bases in DNA contains and conveys the information for the synthesis and assembly of cell components. Some primitive life-forms, however, use RNA in place of DNA as a primary carrier of genetic information. The replication of the genetic material in these organisms must, however, pass through a DNA phase. In general, despite the exceptional diversity of life on Earth, there can be found many remarkable similarities in the genetic codes of nearly all organisms.

The chemical reactions that take place in living cells are similar as well. Green plants use the energy of sunlight to convert water (H_2O) and carbon dioxide (CO_2) to carbohydrates (sugars and starches), other organic (carbon-containing) compounds, and molecular oxygen (O_2). The process of photosynthesis requires energy, in the form of sunlight, to split one water molecule into one-half of an oxygen molecule (O_2; the oxidizing agent) and two hydrogen atoms (H; the reducing agent), each of which dissociates to one hydrogen ion (H^+) and one electron. Through a series of oxidation-reduction reactions, electrons (denoted e^-) are transferred from a donating molecule (oxidation), in this case water, to an accepting molecule (reduction) by a series of chemical reactions. This "reducing power" may be coupled ultimately to the reduction of carbon dioxide to the level of carbohydrate. In effect, carbon dioxide accepts and bonds with hydrogen, forming carbohydrates ($C_n[H_2O]_n$).

Living organisms that require oxygen reverse this process: they consume carbohydrates and other organic materials, using oxygen synthesized by plants to form water, carbon dioxide, and energy. The process that removes hydrogen atoms (containing electrons) from the carbohydrates and passes them to the oxygen is an energy-yielding series of reactions.

In plants, all but two of the steps in the process that converts carbon dioxide to carbohydrates are the same as those steps that synthesize sugars from simpler starting materials in animals, fungi, and bacteria. Similarly, the series of reactions that take a given starting material and synthesize certain molecules that will be used in other synthetic pathways are similar, or identical, among all cell types. From a metabolic point of view, the cellular processes that take place in a lion are only marginally different from those that take place in a dandelion.

BIOLOGICAL ENERGY EXCHANGES

The energy changes associated with physicochemical processes are the province of thermodynamics, a subdiscipline of physics. The first two laws of thermodynamics state, in essence, that energy can be neither created nor destroyed and that the effect of physical and chemical changes is to increase the disorder, or randomness (i.e., entropy), of the universe. Although it might be supposed that biological processes—through which organisms grow in a highly ordered and complex manner, maintain order and complexity throughout their life, and pass on the instructions for order to succeeding generations— are in contravention of these laws, this is not so. Living organisms neither consume nor create energy: they can only transform it from one form to another. From the environment they absorb energy in a form useful to them, and to the environment they return an equivalent amount of energy in a biologically less useful form. The useful energy, or free energy, may be defined as energy capable of doing work under isothermal conditions (conditions in which no temperature differential exists). Free energy is associated with any chemical change. Energy less useful than free energy is returned to the environment, usually as heat. Heat cannot perform work in biological systems because all parts of cells have essentially the same temperature and pressure.

THE CARRIER OF CHEMICAL ENERGY

At any given time, a neutral molecule of water dissociates into a hydrogen ion (H^+) and a hydroxide ion (OH^-), and the ions are continually re-forming into the neutral molecule. Under normal conditions (neutrality), the concentration of hydrogen ions (acidic ions) is equal to that of the hydroxide ions (basic ions), and each ion is present at a concentration of 10^{-7} moles per litre, which is described as a pH of 7.

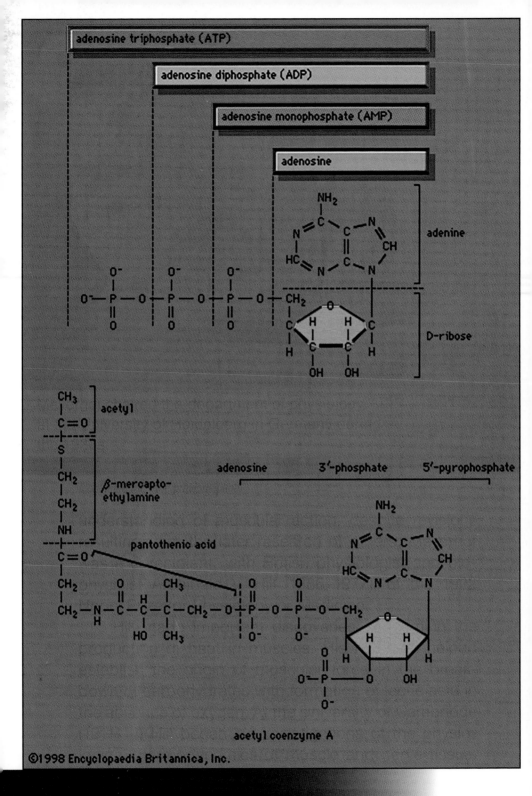

Biological energy carriers

All cells either are bounded by membranes or contain organelles that have membranes. These membranes do not permit water or the ions derived from water to pass into or out of the cells or organelles. In green plants, sunlight is absorbed by chlorophyll and other pigments in the chloroplasts of the cells, called photosystem II. When a water molecule is split by light energy, one-half of an oxygen molecule and two hydrogen atoms (which dissociate to two electrons and two hydrogen ions, H^+) are formed. When excited by sunlight, chlorophyll loses one electron to an electron carrier molecule but quickly recovers it from a hydrogen atom of the split water molecule, which sends H^+ into solution in the process. Two oxygen atoms come together to form a molecule of oxygen gas (O_2). The free electrons are passed to photosystem I, but, in doing so, an excess concentration of positively charged hydrogen ions (H^+) appears on one side of the membrane in the chloroplast, whereas an excess of negatively charged hydroxide ions (OH^-) builds up on the other side. The free energy released as H^+ ions move through a specific "pore" in the membrane, to equalize the concentrations of ions, is sufficient to make some biological processes work, such as the uptake of certain nutrients by bacteria and the rotation of the whiplike protein-based propellers that enable such bacteria to move. Equally important, however, is that this gradient across the membrane powers the formation of ATP from inorganic phosphate (HPO_4^{2-}, abbreviated P_i)) and adenosine diphosphate (ADP). It is ATP that is the major carrier of biologically utilizable energy in all forms of living matter. The interrelationships of energy-yielding and energy-requiring metabolic reactions may be considered largely as processes that couple the formation of ATP with its breakdown.

Synthesis of ATP by green plants is similar to the synthesis of ATP that takes place in the mitochondria of animal, plant, and fungus cells, and in the plasma membranes of bacteria that use oxygen (or other inorganic electron acceptors, such as nitrate) to accept electrons from the removal of hydrogen atoms from a molecule of food. Through these processes most of the energy stored in food materials is released and converted into the molecules that fuel life processes. It must also be remembered, however, that many living organisms (usually bacteria and protozoa) cannot tolerate oxygen. These organisms instead form ATP from inorganic phosphate and ADP by substrate-level phosphorylations (the addition of a phosphate group) that do not involve the establishment and collapse of proton gradients across membranes. It must also be borne in mind that the fuels of life and the cellular "furnace" in which they are "burned" are made of the same types of material: if the fires burn too brightly, not only the fuel but also the furnace is consumed. It is therefore essential to release energy at small, discrete, readily utilizable intervals. The relative complexity of the catabolic pathways (by which food materials are broken down) and the complexity of the anabolic pathways (by which cell components are synthesized) reflect this need and offer the possibility for simple feedback systems to control the rate at which materials travel along these sequences of enzymic reactions.

CATABOLISM

The release of chemical energy from food materials essentially occurs in three phases. In the first phase (phase I), the large molecules that make up the bulk of food materials are broken down into small constituent units: proteins are converted to the 20 or so different amino acids of which they are composed; carbohydrates (polysaccharides such as starch in plants and glycogen in animals) are degraded to sugars such as glucose; and fats (lipids) are broken down into fatty acids and glycerol. The amounts of energy liberated in phase I are relatively small: only about 0.6 percent of the free, or useful, energy of proteins and carbohydrates, and about 0.1 percent of that of fats, is released during this phase. Because this energy is liberated largely as heat, it cannot be utilized by the cell. The purpose of the reactions of phase I, which can be grouped under the term *digestion* and which, in animals, occur mainly in the intestinal tract and in tissues in which reserve materials are prepared, or mobilized, for energy production, is to prepare the foodstuffs for the energy releasing processes.

Incomplete Oxidation

In the second phase of the release of energy from food (phase II), the small molecules produced in the first phase—sugars, glycerol, a number of fatty acids, and about 20 varieties of amino acids—are incompletely oxidized (in this sense, oxidation means the removal of electrons or hydrogen atoms). Thus, the end product (apart from carbon dioxide and water) can be one of only three possible substances: the two-carbon compound acetate, in the form of a compound called acetyl coenzyme A; the four-carbon compound oxaloacetate; and the five-carbon compound α-oxoglutarate. The first, acetate in the form of acetyl coenzyme A, constitutes by far the most common product—it is the product of two-thirds of the carbon incorporated into carbohydrates and glycerol; all of the carbon in most fatty acids; and approximately half of the carbon in amino acids.

The end product of several amino acids is α-oxoglutarate, and that of a few others is oxalo-acetate, which is formed either directly or indirectly

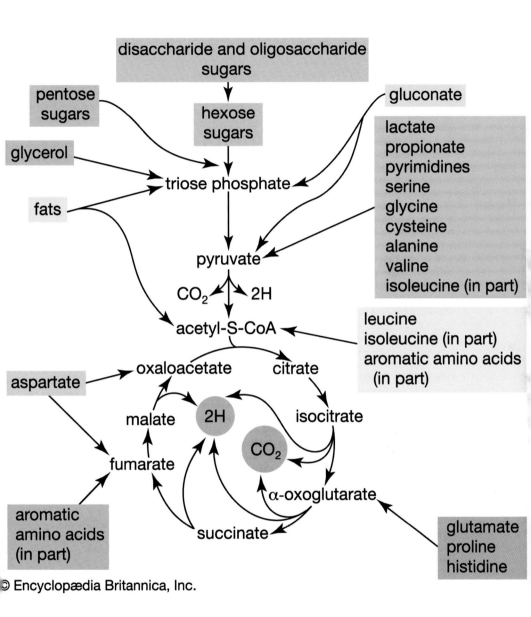

© Encyclopædia Britannica, Inc.

Pathways for the catabolism of nutrients by
Escherichia coli

(from fumarate). These processes take place in the bacterium *Escherichia coli*, but essentially similar processes occur in animals, plants, fungi, and other organisms capable of oxidizing their food materials wholly to carbon dioxide and water.

COMPLETE OXIDATION

Total oxidation of the relatively few products of phase II occurs in a cyclic sequence of chemical reactions known as the tricarboxylic acid (TCA) cycle, or the Krebs cycle, after its discoverer, Sir Hans Krebs.

This cycle represents phase III of energy release from foods. Each turn of this cycle is initiated by the formation of citrate, with six carbon atoms, from oxaloacetate (with four carbons) and acetyl coenzyme A. Subsequent reactions result in the reformation of oxaloacetate and the formation of two molecules of carbon dioxide. The carbon atoms that go into the formation of carbon dioxide are no longer available to the cell. The concomitant stepwise oxidations—in which hydrogen atoms or electrons are removed from intermediate compounds formed during the cycle and, via a system of carriers, are transferred ultimately to oxygen to form water—are quantitatively the most important means of generating ATP from ADP and inorganic phosphate. These events are known as terminal respiration and oxidative phosphorylation.

DISCOVERING THE TCA CYCLE

German-born British biochemist Sir Hans Adolf Krebs (1900–81) received (with Fritz Lipmann) the 1953 Nobel Prize for Physiology or Medicine for the discovery in living organisms of the series of chemical reactions known as the tricarboxylic acid cycle (also called the citric acid cycle, or Krebs cycle). These reactions involve the conversion—in the presence of oxygen—of substances that are formed by the breakdown of sugars, fats, and protein components to carbon dioxide, water, and energy-rich compounds.

In 1937 Krebs demonstrated the existence of a cycle of chemical reactions that combines the end-product of sugar breakdown, later shown to be an "activated" form of the two-carbon acetic acid, with the four-carbon oxaloacetic acid to form citric acid. The cycle regenerates oxaloacetic acid through a series of intermediate compounds while liberating carbon dioxide and electrons that are immediately utilized to form high-energy phosphate bonds in the form of adenosine triphosphate (ATP; the chemical-energy reservoir of the cell). The discovery of the tricarboxylic acid cycle, which is central to nearly all metabolic reactions and the source of two-thirds of the food-derived energy in higher organisms, was of vital importance to a basic understanding of cell metabolism and molecular biology.

(continued on the next page)

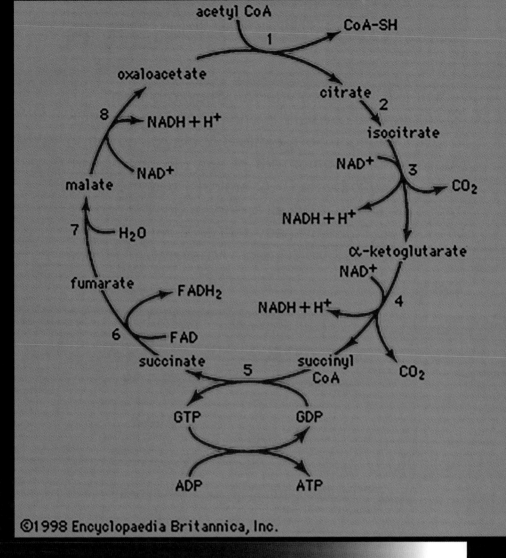

acetyl CoA

CoA-SH

oxaloacetate

1

citrate

2

8

NADH + H$^+$

NAD$^+$

isocitrate

malate

NAD$^+$

3

CO$_2$

7

H$_2$O

NADH + H$^+$

α-ketoglutarate

fumarate

FADH$_2$

NAD$^+$

NADH + H$^+$

4

6

FAD

succinate

5

succinyl
CoA

CO$_2$

GTP

GDP

ADP

ATP

The eight-step tricarboxylic acid cycle

(continued from the previous page)

Although Krebs elucidated most of the reactions in this pathway, there were some gaps in his design. The discovery of coenzyme A in 1945 by Fritz Lipmann and Nathan Kaplan allowed researchers to work out the cycle of reactions as it is known today.

Some microorganisms, incapable of completely converting their carbon compounds to carbon dioxide, release energy by fermentation reactions, in which the intermediate compounds of catabolic routes either directly or indirectly accept or donate hydrogen atoms. Such secondary changes in intermediate compounds result in considerably less energy being made available to the cell than occurs with the pathways that are linked to oxidative phosphorylation. However, fermentation reactions yield a large variety of commercially important products. Thus, for example, if the oxidation (removal of electrons or hydrogen atoms) of some catabolic intermediate is coupled to the reduction of pyruvate or of acetaldehyde derived from pyruvate, the products formed are lactic acid and ethyl alcohol, respectively.

ANABOLISM

Catabolic pathways effect the transformation of food materials into interconvertible intermediates. Anabolic pathways, on the other hand, are sequences of enzyme-catalyzed reactions in which the component building blocks of large molecules, or macromolecules (e.g., proteins, carbohydrates, and fats), are constructed from the same intermediates. Thus, catabolic routes have clearly defined beginnings but no unambiguously identifiable end products, whereas anabolic routes lead to clearly

79

distinguishable end products from diffuse beginnings. The two types of pathway are linked through reactions of phosphate transfer, involving ADP, AMP, and ATP, and also through electron transfers, which enable reducing equivalents (i.e., hydrogen atoms or electrons), which have been released during catabolic reactions, to be utilized for biosynthesis. But, although catabolic and anabolic pathways are closely linked, and although the overall effect of one type of route is obviously the opposite of the other, they have few steps in common. The anabolic pathway for the synthesis of a particular molecule generally starts from intermediate compounds quite different from those produced as a result of catabolism of that molecule. For example, microorganisms catabolize aromatic (i.e., containing a ring, or cyclic, structure) amino acids to acetyl coenzyme A and an intermediate compound of the TCA cycle. The biosynthesis of these amino acids, however, starts with a compound derived from pyruvate and an intermediate compound of the metabolism of pentose (a general name for sugars with five carbon atoms). Similarly, histidine is synthesized from a pentose sugar but is catabolized to α-oxoglutarate.

Even in cases in which a product of catabolism is used in an anabolic pathway, differences emerge. Thus, fatty acids, which are catabolized to acetyl coenzyme A, are synthesized not from acetyl coenzyme A directly but from a derivative of it, malonyl coenzyme A. Furthermore, even enzymes that catalyze apparently identical steps in catabolic and anabolic routes may exhibit different properties. In general, therefore, the way down (catabolism) is different from the way up (anabolism). These differences are important because they allow for the regulation of catabolic and anabolic processes in the cell.

In eukaryotic cells (i.e., those with a well-defined nucleus, characteristic of organisms higher than bacteria) the enzymes of catabolic and anabolic pathways are often located in different cellular compartments. This also contributes to the manner of their cellular control. For example, the formation of acetyl coenzyme A from fatty acids occurs in animal cells in small sausage-shaped components, or organelles, called mitochondria, which also contain the enzymes for terminal respiration and for oxidative phosphorylation. The biosynthesis of fatty acids from acetyl coenzyme A, on the other hand, occurs in the cytoplasm.

INTEGRATION OF CATABOLISM AND ANABOLISM

Possibly the most important means for controlling the flux of metabolites through catabolic and anabolic pathways, and for integrating the numerous different pathways in the cell, is through the regulation of either the activity or the synthesis of key (pacemaker) enzymes. It was recognized in the

1950s, largely from work with microorganisms, that pacemaker enzymes can interact with small molecules at more than one site on the surface of the enzyme molecule. The reaction between an enzyme and its substrate—defined as the compound with which the enzyme acts to form a product—occurs at a specific site on the enzyme known as the catalytic, or active, site. The proper fit between the substrate and the active site is an essential prerequisite for the occurrence of a reaction catalyzed by an enzyme. Interactions at other, so-called regulatory sites on the enzyme, however, do not result in a chemical reaction but cause changes in the shape of the protein. The changes profoundly affect the catalytic properties of the enzyme, either inhibiting or stimulating the rate of the reaction. Modulation of the activity of pacemaker enzymes may be effected by metabolites of the pathway in which the enzyme acts or by those of another pathway. The process may be described as a "fine control" of metabolism. Very small changes in the chemical environment thus produce important and immediate effects on the rates at which individual metabolic processes occur. Most catabolic pathways are regulated by the relative proportions of ATP, ADP, and AMP in the cell. It is reasonable to suppose that a pathway that serves to make ATP available for energy-requiring reactions would be less active if sufficient ATP were already present, than if ADP or AMP were to accumulate. The relative amounts of the adenine nucleotides (i.e., ATP, ADP, and AMP) thus modulate the overall rate of catabolic pathways. They do so by reacting with specific regulatory sites on pacemaker enzymes necessary for the catabolic pathways, which do not participate in the anabolic routes that effect the opposite reactions. Similarly, it is reasonable to suppose that many anabolic processes, which require energy, are inhibited by ADP or AMP. Elevated levels of these nucleotides may be regarded therefore as cellular distress signals indicating a lack of energy.

Since one way in which anabolic pathways differ from catabolic routes is that the former result in identifiable end products, it is not unexpected that the pacemaker enzymes of many anabolic pathways—particularly those effecting the biosynthesis of amino acids and nucleotides—are regulated by the end products of these pathways or, in cases in which branching of pathways occurs, by end products of each branch. Such pacemaker enzymes usually act at the first step unique to a particular anabolic route. If branching occurs, the first step of each branch is controlled. By this so-called negative feedback system, the cellular concentrations of products determine the rates of their formation, thus ensuring that the cell synthesizes only as much of the products as it needs.

A second and less immediately responsive, or "coarse," control is exerted over the synthesis of pacemaker enzymes. The rate of protein synthesis reflects the activity of appropriate genes, which contain the information that directs all cellular processes. Coarse control is therefore exerted on genetic material rather than on enzymes. Preferential synthesis of a pacemaker enzyme is particularly required to accommodate a cell to major changes in its chemical milieu. Such changes occur in multicellular organisms only to a minor extent, so that this type of control mechanism is less important in animals than in microorganisms. In the latter, however, it may determine the ease with which a cell previously growing in one nutrient medium can grow after transfer to another. In cases in which several types of organism compete in the same medium for available carbon sources, the operation of coarse controls may well be decisive in ensuring survival.

Alterations in the differential rates of synthesis of pacemaker enzymes in microorganisms responding to changes in the composition of their growth medium also manifest the properties of negative feedback systems. Depending on the nature of the metabolic pathway of which a pacemaker enzyme is a constituent, the manner in which the alterations are elicited may be distinguished. Thus, an increase in the rates at which enzymes of catabolic routes are synthesized results from the addition of inducers— usually compounds that exhibit some structural similarity to the substrates on which the enzymes act. A classic example of an inducible enzyme of this type is β-galactosidase. *Escherichia coli* growing in nutrient medium containing glucose do not utilize the milk sugar, lactose (glucose-4-β-D-galactoside). However, if the bacteria are placed in a growth medium containing lactose as the sole source of carbon, they synthesize β-galactosidase and can therefore utilize lactose. The reaction catalyzed by the enzyme is the hydrolysis (i.e., breakdown involving water) of lactose to its two constituent sugars, glucose and galactose. The preferential synthesis of the enzyme thus allows the bacteria to use the lactose for growth and energy. Another characteristic of the process of enzyme induction is that it continues only as long as the inducer (in this case, lactose) is present. If cells synthesizing β-galactosidase are transferred to a medium containing no lactose, synthesis of β-galactosidase ceases, and the amount of the enzyme in the cells is diluted as they divide, until the original low level of the enzyme is reestablished.

In contrast, the differential rates of synthesis of pacemaker enzymes of anabolic routes are usually not increased by the presence of inducers. Instead, the absence of small molecules that act to repress enzyme synthesis accelerates enzyme formation. Similar to the fine control processes described earlier is the regulation by coarse control of many pacemaker enzymes of amino-acid biosynthesis. Like the end product inhibitors, the repressors in these cases also appear to be the amino-acid end products themselves.

It is useful to regard the acceleration of the enzyme-forming machinery as the consequence, metaphorically, of either placing a foot on the accelerator or removing it from the brake. Analysis of the mechanisms by which gene activity is controlled suggest, however, that the distinction between inducible and repressible enzymes may be more apparent than real.

METABOLIC PATHWAYS

There are two main reasons for studying a metabolic pathway: (1) to describe, in quantitative terms, the chemical changes catalyzed by the component enzymes of the route; and (2) to describe the various intracellular controls that govern the rate at which the pathway functions. Studies with whole organisms or organs can provide information that one substance is converted to another and that this process is localized in a certain tissue. For example, experiments can show that urea, the chief nitrogen-containing end product of protein metabolism in mammals, is formed exclusively in the liver. They cannot reveal, however, the details of the enzymatic steps involved. Clues to the identity of the products involved, and to the possible chemical changes effected by component enzymes, can be provided in any of four ways involving studies with either whole organisms or tissues.

First, under stress or the imbalances associated with diseases, certain metabolites may accumulate to a greater extent than normal. Thus, during the stress of violent exercise, lactic acid appears in the blood, while glycogen, the form in which carbohydrate is stored in muscle, disappears. Such observations do not, however, prove that lactic acid is a normal intermediate of glycogen catabolism. Rather, they show only that compounds capable of yielding lactic acid are likely to be normal intermediates. Indeed, in the example, lactic acid is formed in response to abnormal circumstances and is not directly formed in the pathways of carbohydrate catabolism. On the other hand, the abnormal accumulation of pyruvic acid in the blood of vitamin B_1-deficient pigeons was a valuable clue to the role of this vitamin in the oxidation of pyruvate.

Second, the administration of metabolic poisons may lead to the accumulation of specific metabolites. If fluoroacetic acid or fluorocitric acid is ingested by animals, for example, citric acid accumulates in the liver. This correctly suggests that fluorocitric acid administered as such, or formed from fluoroacetic acid via the tricarboxylic acid (TCA) cycle, inhibits an enzyme of citrate oxidation.

Third, the fate of any nutrient—indeed, often the fate of a particular chemical group or atom in a nutrient—can be followed with relative ease by administering the nutrient labeled with an isotope. Isotopes are forms of an element that are chemically indistinguishable from each other but differ in physical properties.

The use of a nonradioactive isotope of nitrogen in the 1930s first revealed the dynamic state of body constituents. It had previously been believed that the proteins of tissues are stable once formed, disappearing only with the death of the cell. By feeding amino acids labeled with isotopic nitrogen to rats, it was discovered that the isotope was incorporated into many of the amino acids found in proteins of the liver and the gut, even though the total protein content of these tissues did not change. This suggested that the proteins of these tissues exist in a dynamic steady state, in which relatively high rates of synthesis are counterbalanced by equal rates of degradation. Thus, although the average liver cell has a life-span of several months, half of its proteins are synthesized and degraded every five to six days. On the other hand, the proteins of the muscle or the brain, tissues that (unlike the gut or liver) need not adjust to changes in the chemical composition of their milieu, do not turn over as rapidly. The high rates of turnover observed in liver and gut tissues indicate that the coarse controls, exerted through the onset and cessation of synthesis of pacemaker enzymes, do occur in animal cells.

Finally, organisms carrying genetic mutations may fail to synthesize certain enzymes in an active form. Such defects, if not lethal, result in the accumulation and excretion of the substrate of the defective enzyme. In normal organisms, the substrate would not accumulate, because it would be acted upon by the enzyme. The significance of this observation was first realized in the early 20th century when the phrase "inborn errors of metabolism" was used to describe hereditary conditions in which a variety of amino acids and other metabolites are excreted in the urine. In microorganisms, in which it is relatively easy to cause genetic mutations and to select specific mutants, this technique has been very useful. In addition to their utility in the unraveling of metabolic pathways, the use of mutants in the early 1940s led to the postulation of the one gene-one enzyme hypothesis by the Nobel Prize winners George Wells Beadle and Edward L. Tatum. Their discoveries opened the field of biochemical genetics and first revealed the nature of the fine controls of metabolism.

Because detailed information about the mechanisms of component enzymatic steps in any metabolic pathway cannot be obtained from studies with whole organisms or tissues, various techniques have been developed for studying these processes—e.g., sliced tissues, and homogenates and cell-free extracts, which are produced by physical disruption of the cells and the removal of cell walls and other

THE ONE-GENE–ONE-ENZYME HYPOTHESIS

George Wells Beadle (1903–1989) and Edward L. Tatum (1909–1975) helped found biochemical genetics when they showed that genes affect heredity by determining enzyme structure. They shared the 1958 Nobel Prize for Physiology or Medicine with Joshua Lederberg, who discovered the mechanisms of genetic recombination in bacteria.

Beadle and Tatum conducted their studies in the pink bread mold *Neurospora crassa*. Their experiments involved first exposing the mold to mutation-inducing X-rays and then culturing it in a minimal growth medium that contained only the basic nutrients that the wild-type, or nonmutated, strain of mold needed to survive. They found that the mutant strains of mold required the addition of specific amino acids to the minimal medium in order to grow. Using this information, the researchers were able to associate mutations in specific genes to the disruption of individual enzymes in the metabolic pathways that normally produced the missing amino acids. Thus, they showed that each gene in some way determines the structure of a specific enzyme (the one-gene–one-enzyme hypothesis).

Although the hypothesis was amply verified in principle, it has undergone considerable sophistication since the 1940s. Today it is known that not all genes encode an enzyme and that some enzymes are made up of several short polypeptides encoded by two or more genes.

debris. The sliced-tissue technique was successfully used by the Nobel Prize winner Sir Hans Krebs in his pioneer studies in the early 1930s on the mechanism of urea formation in the liver. Measurements were made of the stimulating effects of small quantities of amino acids on both the rate of oxygen uptake and the amount of oxygen taken up. The amino acids were added to liver slices bathed in a nutrient medium. Such measurements revealed the cyclic nature of the process, in which specific amino acids acted as catalysts, stimulating respiration to an extent greater than expected from the quantities added. This was because the added material had been re-formed in the course of the cycle.

Homogenates of tissue are useful in studying metabolic processes because permeability barriers that may prevent ready access of external materials to cell components are destroyed. The tissue is usually minced, blended, or otherwise disrupted in a medium that is suitably buffered to maintain the normal acid–base balance of the tissue, and contains the ions required for many life processes, chiefly sodium, potassium, and magnesium. The tissue is either used directly—as was done by Krebs in elucidating, in 1937, the TCA cycle from studies of the respiration of minced pigeon breast muscle—or fractionated (i.e., broken down) further. If the latter procedure is followed, homogenization is often carried out in a medium containing a high concentration of the sugar sucrose, which provides an environment favourable for maintaining the integrity of cellular components. The components are recovered by careful spinning in a centrifuge, at a series of increasing speeds. It is thus possible to obtain fractions containing predominantly one type of organelle: nuclei (and some unbroken cells); mitochondria, lysosomes, and microbodies; microsomes (i.e., ribosomes and endoplasmic reticulum fragments); and—after prolonged centrifugation at forces in excess of 100,000 times gravity—a clear liquid that represents the soluble fraction of the cytoplasm. The fractions thus obtained can be further purified and tested for their capacity to carry out a given metabolic step or steps. This procedure was used to show that isolated mitochondria catalyze the oxidation reactions of the TCA cycle and that these organelles also contain the enzymes of fatty acid oxidation. Similarly, isolated ribosomes are used to study the pathway and mechanism of protein synthesis.

The final step in elucidating a reaction in a metabolic pathway includes isolation of the enzyme involved. The rate of the reaction and the factors that control the activity of the enzyme are then measured. It should be emphasized that biochemists realize that studies on isolated and highly purified systems can do no more than approximate biological reality. The identification of the fine and coarse controls of a metabolic pathway, and (when appropriate) other influences on that pathway, must ultimately involve the study of the pathway in the whole cell or organism. Although some techniques have proved adequate for relating findings in the test tube to the situation in living organisms, study of the more complex metabolic processes, such as those involved in differentiation and development, may require the elaboration of new experimental approaches.

CHAPTER

3

CATABOLISM OF SUGARS, LIPIDS, AND PROTEINS

F ood materials must undergo oxidation in order to yield biologically useful energy. Oxidation does not necessarily involve oxygen, although it must involve the transfer of electrons from a donor molecule to a suitable acceptor molecule. The donor is thus oxidized and the recipient reduced. Many microorganisms either must live in the absence of oxygen (i.e., are obligate anaerobes) or can live in its presence or its absence (i.e., are facultative anaerobes).

If no oxygen is available, the catabolism of food materials is effected via fermentations, in which the final acceptor of the electrons removed from the nutrient is some organic molecule, usually generated during the fermentation process. There is no net oxidation of the food molecule in this type of catabolism—the overall oxidation state of the fermentation products is the same as that of the starting material. Organisms that can use oxygen as a final electron acceptor also use many of the steps in the fermentation pathways in which food molecules are broken down to smaller fragments. These fragments, instead of serving as electron acceptors, are fed into the TCA cycle, the pathway of terminal respiration.

In this cycle all of the hydrogen atoms or electrons (e^-) are removed from the fragments and are channeled through a series of electron carriers, ultimately to react with oxygen. All carbon atoms are eliminated as carbon dioxide (CO_2) in this process. The sequence of reactions involved in the catabolism of food materials may thus be conveniently considered in terms of an initial fragmentation (fermentation), followed by a combustion (respiration) process.

GLUCOSE CATABOLISM

Quantitatively, the most important source of energy for cellular processes is the six-carbon sugar glucose ($C_6H_{12}O_6$). Glucose is made available to animals through the hydrolysis of polysaccharides, such as glycogen and starch, the process being catalyzed by digestive enzymes. In animals, the sugar thus set free passes from the gut into the bloodstream and from there into the cells of the liver and other tissues. In microorganisms, of course, no such specialized tissues are involved.

The fermentative phase of glucose catabolism (glycolysis) involves several enzymes. In living cells many of the compounds that take part in metabolism exist as negatively charged moieties, or anions (e.g., pyruvate, oxaloacetate). In order to obtain a net yield of ATP from the catabolism of glucose, it is first necessary to invest ATP. During step [1], the alcohol group at position 6 of the glucose molecule readily reacts with the terminal phosphate group of ATP, forming glucose 6-phosphate and ADP. (For convenience, in the following reactions, the phosphoryl group $[PO_3^{2-}]$ is represented by encircled P.)

Because the decrease in free energy is so large, this reaction is virtually irreversible under physiological conditions.

In animals, this phosphorylation of glucose, which yields glucose 6-phosphate, is catalyzed by two different enzymes. In most cells a hexokinase with a high affinity for glucose—i.e., only small amounts of glucose are necessary for enzymatic activity—effects the reaction.

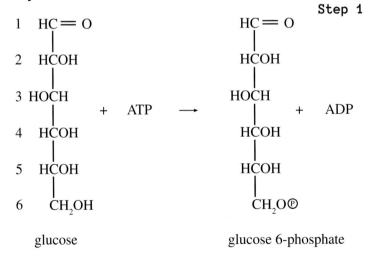

Step 1

glucose $\quad$ glucose 6-phosphate

In addition, the liver contains a glucokinase, which requires a much greater concentration of glucose before it reacts. Glucokinase functions only in emergencies, when the concentration of glucose in the blood rises to abnormally high levels.

Certain facultative anaerobic bacteria also contain hexokinases but apparently do not use them to phosphorylate glucose. In such cells, external glucose can be utilized only if it is first phosphorylated to glucose 6-phosphate via a system linked to the cell membrane that involves a compound called phosphoenolpyruvate, which serves as an obligatory donor of the phosphate group; i.e., ATP cannot serve as the phosphate donor in the reaction.

The reaction in which glucose 6-phosphate is changed to fructose 6-phosphate is catalyzed by phosphoglucoisomerase. In the reaction, a secondary alcohol group at the second carbon atom is oxidized to a ketogroup, and the aldehyde group (-CHO) at the first carbon atom is reduced to a primary alcohol group ($-CH_2OH$). This reaction is readily reversible, as is indicated by the double arrows.

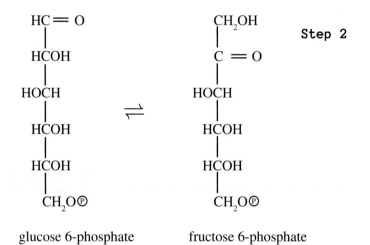

glucose 6-phosphate   fructose 6-phosphate

The formation of the alcohol group at the first carbon atom permits the repetition of the reaction effected in step [1]—that is, a second molecule of ATP is invested. The product is fructose 1,6-diphosphate (see steps [3]). Again, as in the hexokinase reaction, the decrease in free energy of the reaction, which is catalyzed by phosphofructokinase, is sufficiently large to make this reaction virtually irreversible under physiological conditions. ADP is also a product.

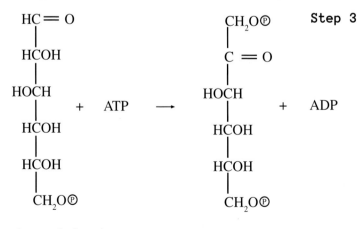

glucose 6-phosphate   fructose 1,6-diphosphate

98

The first three steps of glycolysis have thus transformed an asymmetrical sugar molecule, glucose, into a symmetrical form, fructose 1,6-diphosphate, containing a phosphoryl group at each end. The molecule next is split into two smaller fragments that are interconvertible. This elegant simplification is achieved via steps [4] and [5].

Step 4

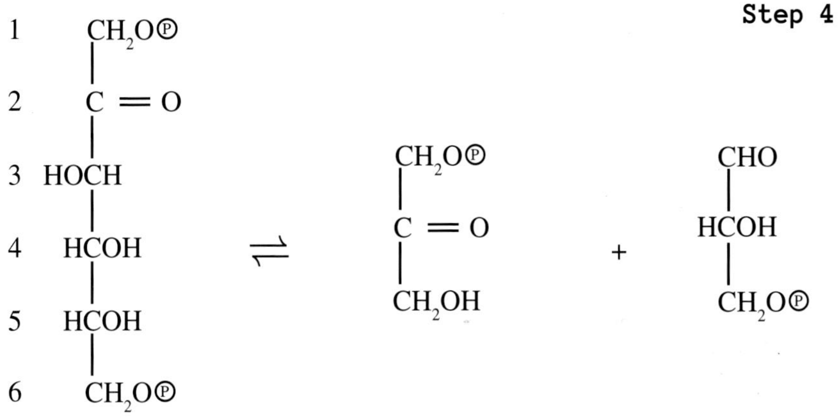

$$
\begin{array}{llll}
1 & CH_2O\circledP & & \\
2 & C = O & & \\
3 & HOCH & & CH_2O\circledP & CHO \\
4 & HCOH & \rightleftharpoons & C = O & + \quad HCOH \\
5 & HCOH & & CH_2OH & CH_2O\circledP \\
6 & CH_2O\circledP & & &
\end{array}
$$

fructose 1,6-diphosphate   dihydroxyacetone phosphate   glyceraldehyde 3-phosphate

Step 5

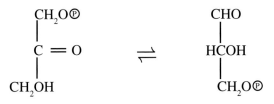

$$
\begin{array}{ccc}
CH_2O\circledP & & CHO \\
C = O & \rightleftharpoons & HCOH \\
CH_2OH & & CH_2O\circledP
\end{array}
$$

dihydroxyacetone phosphate   glyceraldehyde 3-phosphate

99

THE ALDOLASE REACTION

In step [4], an enzyme catalyzes the breaking apart of the six-carbon sugar fructose 1,6-diphosphate into two three-carbon fragments. The molecule is split between carbons 3 and 4. Reversal of this cleavage—i.e., the formation of a six-carbon compound from two three-carbon compounds—is possible. Because the reverse reaction is an aldol condensation—i.e., an aldehyde (glyceraldehyde 3-phosphate) combines with a ketone (dihydroxyacetone phosphate)—the enzyme is commonly called aldolase. The two three-carbon fragments produced in step [4], dihydroxyacetone phosphate and glyceraldehyde 3-phosphate, are also called triose phosphates. They are readily converted to each other by a process shown in step [5] analogous to that in step [2]. The enzyme that catalyzes the interconversion [5] is triose phosphate isomerase, a different enzyme than that catalyzing step [2].

THE FORMATION OF ATP

The second stage of glucose catabolism comprises reactions [6] through [10], in which a net gain of ATP is achieved through the oxidation of one of the triose phosphate compounds formed in step [5]. One molecule of glucose forms two molecules of the triose phosphate. Both three-carbon fragments follow the

RESEARCH ON MUSCLE METABOLISM

In the early 20th century, several scientists made discoveries that contributed to the understanding of how metabolism and heat function in muscle.

German physiological chemist Gustav Georg Embden (1874–1933) conducted studies on the chemistry of carbohydrate metabolism and muscle contraction and was the first to discover and link together all the steps involved in the conversion of glycogen to lactic acid. His studies in the newly developing field of physiological chemistry were primarily concerned with chemical processes in living organisms, especially intermediate metabolic processes in liver tissue. By developing a technique to prevent tissue damage, he discovered the important role of the liver in metabolism and did preliminary studies that led to the investigation of normal sugar metabolism and of its pathological form, diabetes.

Embden and his co-workers isolated several intermediate metabolic products from muscle tissue and discovered the important metabolic compound adenyl phosphoric acid, which is more commonly known as adenosine triphosphate (ATP). In all his work he emphasized the relationships between his results and general cellular processes.

German biochemist Otto Meyerhof (1884–1951) was known for his research on the chemical reactions of metabolism in muscle. His work on the glycogen-lactic acid cycle remains a basic contribution to the

(continued on the next page)

Meyerhof chaired the department of physiology at the University of Heidelberg in Germany during the 1930s.

(continued from the previous page)

understanding of muscular action, despite revisions resulting from the later research of others. Meyerhof was a corecipient, with British physiologist and biophysicist Archibald V. Hill (1886–1977), of the 1922 Nobel Prize for Physiology or Medicine.

Hill made important discoveries concerning the production of heat in muscles. His research helped establish the origin of muscular force in the breakdown of carbohydrates with formation of lactic acid in the absence of oxygen. At the University of Cambridge (1911–14) Hill began his investigations of the physiological thermodynamics of muscle and nerve tissue.

Working with a straplike thigh muscle in the frog, he was able to demonstrate that oxygen is needed only for the recovery, not the contractile, phase of muscular activity, laying the foundation for the discovery of the series of biochemical reactions carried out in muscle cells that results in contraction.

Hill also derived a mathematical expression—known as the "Hill equation"—for the uptake of oxygen by hemoglobin. He returned to scientific research following World War II and continued to publish valuable papers on muscle physiology that are still cited by researchers today.

same pathway, and steps [6] through [10] must occur twice to complete the glucose breakdown.

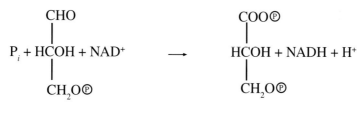

glyceraldehyde 3-phosphate   1,3-diphosphoglycerate

Step [6], in which glyceraldehyde 3-phosphate is oxidized, is one of the most important reactions in glycolysis. It is during this step that the energy liberated during oxidation of the aldehyde group (-CHO) is conserved in the form of a high-energy phosphate compound—namely, as 1,3-diphosphoglycerate, an anhydride of a carboxylic acid and phosphoric acid. The hydrogen atoms or electrons removed from the aldehyde group during its oxidation are accepted by a coenzyme (so called because it functions in conjunction with an enzyme) involved in hydrogen or electron transfer. The coenzyme, nicotinamide adenine dinucleotide (NAD^+), is reduced to form $NADH + H^+$ in the process. The NAD^+ thus reduced is bound to the enzyme glyceraldehyde 3-phosphate dehydrogenase, catalyzing the overall reaction, step [6].

The 1,3-diphosphoglycerate produced in step [6] reacts with ADP in a reaction catalyzed by phosphoglycerate kinase, with the result that one of the two phosphoryl groups is transferred to ADP to form ATP and 3-phosphoglycerate. This reaction [7] is highly exergonic (i.e., it proceeds with a loss of free energy). As a result, the oxidation of glyceraldehyde 3-phosphate (step [6]) is irreversible. In summary, the energy liberated during oxidation of an aldehyde group (-CHO in glyceraldehyde 3-phosphate) to a carboxylic acid group (-COO in 3-phosphoglycerate) is conserved as the phosphate bond energy in ATP during steps [6] and [7]. This step occurs twice for each molecule of glucose, and thus the initial investment of ATP in steps [1] and [3] is recovered.

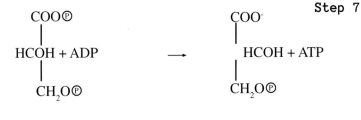

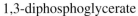

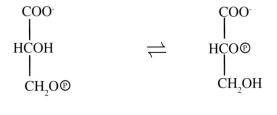

The 3-phosphoglycerate in step [7] now forms 2-phosphoglycerate, in a reaction catalyzed by phosphoglyceromutase [8]. During step [9] the enzyme enolase reacts with 2-phosphoglycerate to form phosphoenolpyruvate (PEP), water being lost from 2-phosphoglycerate in the process. Phosphoenolpyruvate acts as the second source of ATP in glycolysis. The transfer of the phosphate group from PEP to ADP, catalyzed by pyruvate kinase [10], is also highly exergonic and is thus virtually irreversible under physiological conditions.

Step 9

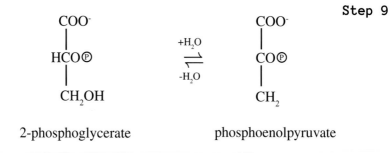

2-phosphoglycerate   phosphoenolpyruvate

Reaction [10] occurs twice for each molecule of glucose entering the glycolytic sequence. Thus, the net yield is two molecules of ATP for each six-carbon sugar.

Step 10

phosphoenolpyruvate   pyruvate

No further molecules of glucose can enter the glycolytic pathway, however, until the $NADH + H^+$ produced in step [6] is reoxidized to NAD^+. In anaerobic systems this means that electrons must be transferred from ($NADH + H^+$) to some organic acceptor molecule, which thus is reduced in the process. Such an acceptor molecule could be the pyruvate formed in reaction [10]. In certain bacteria (e.g., so-called lactic acid bacteria) or in muscle cells functioning vigorously in the absence of adequate supplies of oxygen, pyruvate is reduced to lactate via a reaction catalyzed by lactate dehydrogenase (reaction [11a]).

Step 11a

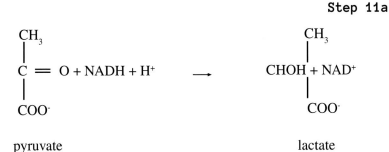

$$\begin{array}{ccc} CH_3 & & CH_3 \\ | & & | \\ C = O + NADH + H^+ & \longrightarrow & CHOH + NAD^+ \\ | & & | \\ COO^- & & COO^- \end{array}$$

pyruvate   lactate

In other words, NADH gives up its hydrogen atoms or electrons to pyruvate, and lactate and NAD^+ are formed. Alternatively, in organisms such as brewers' yeast, pyruvate is first decarboxylated to form acetaldehyde and carbon dioxide in a reaction catalyzed by pyruvate decarboxylase [11b].

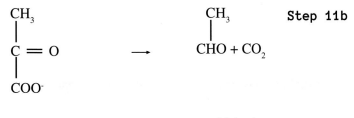

$$\begin{array}{ccc} CH_3 & & CH_3 \qquad \text{Step 11b} \\ | & & | \\ C = O & \longrightarrow & CHO + CO_2 \\ | & & \\ COO^- & & \end{array}$$

pyruvate   acetaldehyde

Acetaldehyde then is reduced (by $NADH + H^+$) in a reaction catalyzed by alcohol dehydrogenase [11c], yielding ethanol and oxidized coenzyme (NAD^+).

$$\underset{|}{CH_3} + NADH + H^+ \longrightarrow CH_3CH_2OH + NAD^+$$
$$CHO$$

acetaldehyde   ethanol

Many variations of reactions [11a, b, and c] occur in nature. In the heterolactic (mixed lactic acid) fermentations carried out by some microorganisms, a mixture of reactions [11a, b, and c] regenerates NAD^+ and results in the production, for each molecule of glucose fermented, of a molecule each of lactate, ethanol, and carbon dioxide. In other types of fermentation, the end products may be derivatives of acids such as propionic, butyric, acetic, and succinic; decarboxylated materials derived from them (e.g., acetone); or compounds such as glycerol.

THE PHOSPHOGLUCONATE PATHWAY

Many cells possess, in addition to all or part of the glycolytic pathway that comprises reactions [1 through 11], other pathways of glucose catabolism that involve, as the first unique step, the oxidation of glucose 6-phosphate [12] instead of the formation of fructose 6-phosphate [2]. This is the phosphogluconate pathway, or pentose phosphate cycle.

During reaction [12], hydrogen atoms or electrons are removed from the carbon atom at position 1 of glucose 6-phosphate in a reaction catalyzed by glucose 6-phosphate dehydrogenase. The product of the reaction is 6-phosphogluconate.

Step 12

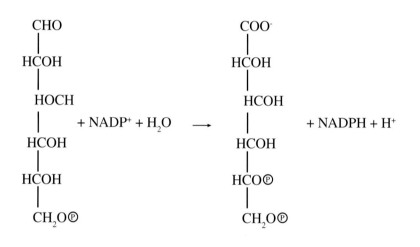

The reducing equivalents (hydrogen atoms or electrons) are accepted by nicotine adenine dinucleotide phosphate ($NADP^+$), a coenzyme similar to but not identical with NAD^+. A second molecule of $NADP^+$ is reduced as 6-phosphogluconate is further oxidized. The reaction is catalyzed by 6-phosphogluconate dehydrogenase [13]. The products of the reaction also include ribulose 5-phosphate and carbon dioxide. (The numbers at the carbon atoms in step [13] indicate that carbon 1 of 6-phosphogluconate forms carbon dioxide.)

Step 13

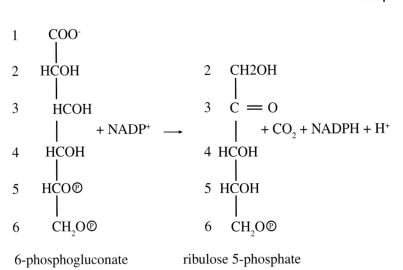

6-phosphogluconate   ribulose 5-phosphate

Ribulose 5-phosphate can undergo a series of reactions in which two-carbon and three-carbon fragments are interchanged between a number of sugar phosphates. This sequence of events can lead to the formation of two molecules of fructose 6-phosphate and one of glyceraldehyde 3-phosphate from three molecules of ribulose 5-phosphate (i.e., the conversion of three molecules with five carbons to two with six and one with three). Although the cycle, which is outlined in Figure 4, is the main pathway in microorganisms for fragmentation of pentose sugars, it is not of major importance as a route for the oxidation of

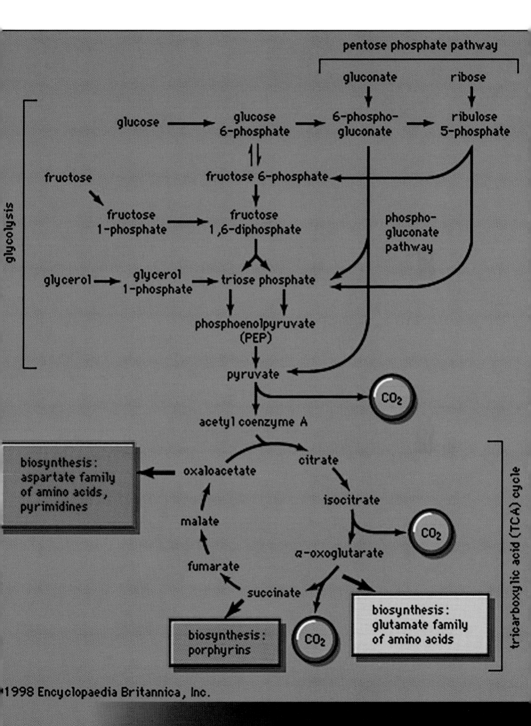

Pathways for the utilization of carbohydrates

glucose. Its primary purpose in most cells is to generate reducing power in the cytoplasm, in the form of reduced $NADP^+$. This function is especially prominent in tissues—such as the liver, mammary gland, fat tissue, and the cortex (outer region) of the adrenal gland—that actively carry out the biosynthesis of fatty acids and other fatty substances (e.g., steroids). A second function of reactions [12] and [13] is to generate from glucose 6-phosphate the pentoses that are used in the synthesis of nucleic acids.

In photosynthetic organisms, some of the reactions of the phosphogluconate pathway are part of the major route for the formation of sugars from carbon dioxide. In this case, the reactions occur in a direction opposite to that in which they occur in nonphotosynthetic tissues.

A different route for the catabolism of glucose also involves 6-phosphogluconate. This route is of considerable importance in microorganisms lacking some of the enzymes necessary for glycolysis. In this route, 6-phosphogluconate (derived from glucose via steps [1] and [12]) is not oxidized to ribulose 5-phosphate via reaction [13] but, in an enzyme-catalyzed reaction [14], loses water, forming the compound 2-keto-3-deoxy-6-phosphogluconate (KDPG).

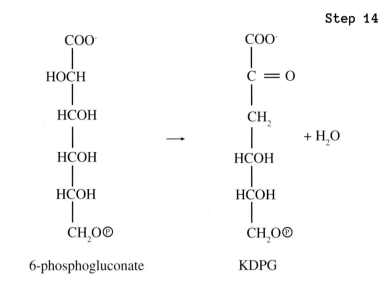

Step 14

6-phosphogluconate → KDPG + H_2O

This is then split into pyruvate and glyceraldehyde 3-phosphate [15], both of which are intermediates of the glycolytic pathway.

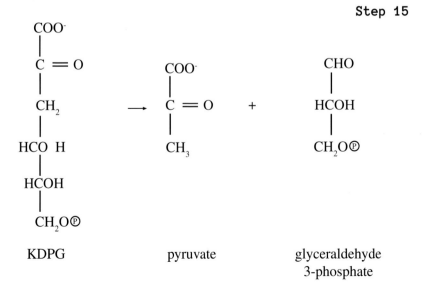

Step 15

KDPG → pyruvate + glyceraldehyde 3-phosphate

113

CATABOLISM OF OTHER SUGARS

The main storage carbohydrate of animal cells is glycogen, in which chains of glucose molecules—linked end-to-end, the C1 position of one glucose being linked to the C4 position of the adjacent one—are joined to each other by occasional linkages between a carbon at position 1 on one glucose and a carbon at position 6 on another. Two enzymes cooperate in releasing glucose molecules from glycogen. Glycogen phosphorylase catalyzes the splitting of the 1,4-bonds by adding the elements of phosphoric acid at the point shown by the broken arrow in [16], rather than water, as in the digestive hydrolysis of polysaccharides such as glycogen and starch. The products of [16] are glucose 1-phosphate and chains of sugar molecules shortened by one unit. The chains are degraded further by repetition of step [16]. When a bridge linking two chains, at C1 and C6 carbon atoms of adjacent glucose units, is reached, it is hydrolyzed in a reaction involving the enzyme α $(1 \rightarrow 6)$ glucosidase. After the two chains are separated, reaction [16] can occur again. The glucose 1-phosphate thus formed from glycogen or, in plants, from starch, is converted to glucose 6-phosphate by phosphoglucomutase, which catalyzes a reaction very similar to that effected in step [8] of glycolysis. Glucose 6-phosphate can then undergo further catabolism via glycolysis [reactions 2 through 10] or via either

114

of the routes involving formation of 6-phosphoglu-conate [12].

Other sugars encountered in the diet are likewise transformed to products that are intermediates of central metabolic pathways. Lactose, or milk sugar, is composed of one molecule of galactose linked to one molecule of glucose.

Step 16

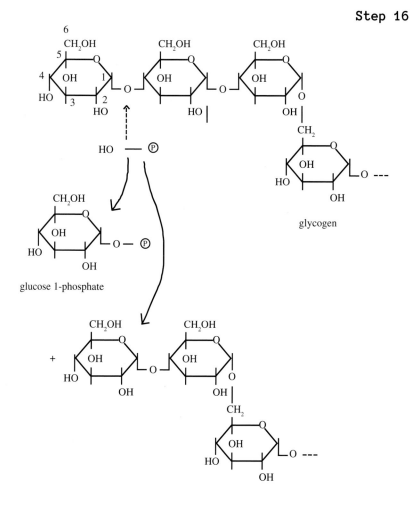

glucose 1-phosphate

glycogen

Sucrose, the common sugar of cane or beet, is made up of glucose linked to fructose. Both sucrose and lactose are hydrolyzed to glucose and fructose or galactose, respectively. Glucose is utilized as already described, but special reactions must occur before the other sugars can enter the catabolic routes. Galactose, for example, is phosphorylated in a manner analogous to step [1] of glycolysis. The reaction, catalyzed by a galactokinase, results in the formation of galactose 1-phosphate. This product is transformed to glucose 1-phosphate by a sequence of reactions requiring as a coenzyme uridine triphosphate (UTP). Fructose may also be phosphorylated in animal cells through the action of hexokinase [1], in which case fructose 6-phosphate is the product, or in liver tissue via a fructokinase that gives rise to fructose 1-phosphate [17]. Adenosine triphosphate supplies the phosphate group in both cases.

Step 17

$$CH_2OH$$
$$|$$
$$C = O$$
$$|$$
$$HCOH$$
$$|$$
$$HCOH$$
$$|$$
$$HCOH$$
$$|$$
$$CH_2OH$$

+ ATP →

$$CH_2O\circledP$$
$$|$$
$$C = O$$
$$|$$
$$HOCH$$
$$|$$
$$HCOH$$
$$|$$
$$HCOH$$
$$|$$
$$CH_2OH$$

+ ADP

fructose   fructose 1-phosphate

Fructose 1-phosphate is also formed when facultative anaerobic microorganisms use fructose as a carbon source for growth. In this case, however, the source of the phosphate is phosphoenolpyruvate rather than ATP. Fructose 1-phosphate can be catabolized by one of two routes. In the liver, it is split by an aldolase enzyme [18] abundant in that tissue (but lacking in muscle), giving the products dihydroxyacetone phosphate and glyceraldehyde. It will be recalled that dihydroxyacetone phosphate is an intermediate compound of glycolysis. Although glyceraldehyde is not an intermediate of glycolysis, it can be converted to one (glyceraldehyde 3-phosphate) in a reaction involving the conversion of ATP to ADP.

Step 18

$$
\begin{array}{c}
CH_2O\text{\textcircled{P}} \\
| \\
C = O \\
| \\
HOCH \\
| \\
HCOH \\
| \\
HCOH \\
| \\
CH_2OH
\end{array}
\quad \rightleftharpoons \quad
\begin{array}{c}
CH_2O\text{\textcircled{P}} \\
| \\
C = O \\
| \\
CH_2OH
\end{array}
\quad + \quad
\begin{array}{c}
CHO \\
| \\
HCOH \\
| \\
CH_2OH
\end{array}
$$

fructose 1-phosphate   dihydroxyacetone   glyceraldehyde
                                    phosphate

In many organisms other than mammals, fructose 1-phosphate does not have to undergo reaction [18] in order to enter central metabolic routes. Instead, a fructose 1-phosphate kinase, distinct from the phosphofructokinase that catalyzes step [3] of glycolysis, effects the direct conversion of fructose 1-phosphate and ATP to fructose 1,6-diphosphate and ADP.

CATABOLISM OF LIPIDS

Although carbohydrates are the major fuel for most organisms, fatty acids are also a very important energy source. In vertebrates at least half of the oxidative energy used by the liver, kidneys, heart muscle, and resting skeletal muscle is derived from the oxidation of fatty acids. In fasting or hibernating animals or in migrating birds, fat is virtually the sole source of energy.

Neutral fats or triglycerides, the major components of storage fats in plant and animal cells, consist of the alcohol glycerol linked to three molecules of fatty acids. Before a molecule of neutral fat can be metabolized, it must be hydrolyzed to its component parts. Hydrolysis [19] is effected by intracellular enzymes or gut enzymes, and forms phase I of fat catabolism. Letters x, y, and z represent the number of $-CH_2-$ groups in the fatty acid molecules.

Step 19

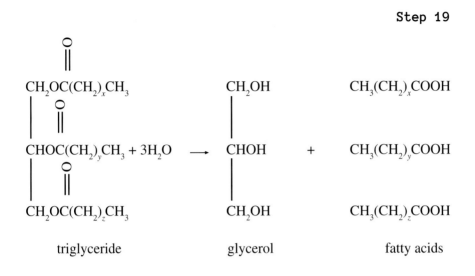

$$CH_2OC(CH_2)_xCH_3$$
$$CHOC(CH_2)_yCH_3 + 3H_2O \longrightarrow$$
$$CH_2OC(CH_2)_zCH_3$$

triglyceride

$$CH_2OH$$
$$CHOH \quad +$$
$$CH_2OH$$

glycerol

$$CH_3(CH_2)_xCOOH$$
$$CH_3(CH_2)_yCOOH$$
$$CH_3(CH_2)_zCOOH$$

fatty acids

As is apparent from [19], the three molecules of fatty acid released from the triglyceride need not be identical. A fatty acid usually contains 16 or 18 carbon atoms but may also be unsaturated—containing one or more double bonds (-CH=CH-). Only the fate of saturated fatty acids, of the type $CH_3(CH_2)_n$ COOH (n most commonly is an even number), is dealt with here.

GLYCEROL

It requires but two reactions to channel glycerol into a catabolic pathway. In a reaction catalyzed by glycerolkinase, ATP is used to phosphorylate glycerol. The products of this reaction are glycerol 1-phosphate and ADP. Glycerol 1-phosphate is then oxidized to dihydroxyacetone phosphate [20], an intermediate of glycolysis. The reaction is catalyzed by either a soluble (cytoplasmic) enzyme, glycerolphosphate dehydrogenase, or a similar enzyme present in the mitochondria. In addition to their different locations, the two dehydrogenase enzymes differ in that a different coenzyme accepts the electrons removed from glycerol 1-phosphate.

Step 20

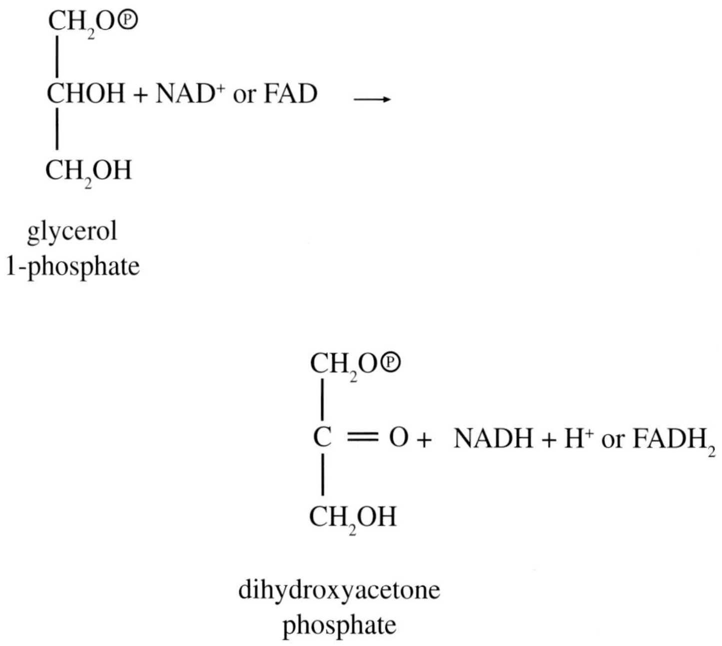

$$
\begin{array}{l}
CH_2O\textcircled{P} \\
| \\
CHOH + NAD^+ \text{ or } FAD \longrightarrow \\
| \\
CH_2OH
\end{array}
$$

glycerol
1-phosphate

$$
\begin{array}{l}
CH_2O\textcircled{P} \\
| \\
C = O + \ NADH + H^+ \text{ or } FADH_2 \\
| \\
CH_2OH
\end{array}
$$

dihydroxyacetone
phosphate

In the case of the cytoplasmic enzyme, NAD^+ accepts the electrons (and is reduced to $NADH + H^+$). In the case of the mitochondrial enzyme, flavin adenine dinucleotide (FAD) accepts the electrons (and is reduced to $FADH_2$).

FATTY ACIDS

As with sugars, the release of energy from fatty acids necessitates an initial investment of ATP. A problem unique to fats is a consequence of the low solubility in water of most fatty acids. Their catabolism requires mechanisms that fragment them in a controlled and stepwise manner. The mechanism involves a coenzyme for the transfer of an acyl group, namely, coenzyme A. The functional portion of this complex molecule is the sulfhydryl (–SH) group at one end. The coenzyme is often identified as CoA–SH (see step [21]). The organized and stepwise degradation of fatty acids linked to coenzyme A is ensured because the necessary enzymes are sequestered in particulate structures. In microorganisms these enzymes are associated with cell membranes, and in higher organisms with mitochondria.

Step 21

$$CH_3(CH_2)_nCOOH + ATP + CoA\text{–}SH \longrightarrow$$

fatty acid

$$CH_3(CH_2)_n\overset{\displaystyle O}{\overset{\displaystyle \|}{C}}S\text{–}CoA + AMP + PP_i$$

fatty acyl
coenzyme A

121

Fatty acids are linked to coenzyme A (CoA–SH) in one of two main ways. In higher organisms, enzymes in the cytoplasm called thiokinases catalyze the linkage of fatty acids with CoA–SH to form a compound that can be called a fatty acyl coenzyme A [21]. This step requires ATP, which is split to AMP and inorganic pyrophosphate (PP$_i$) in the process.

In this series of reactions, n indicates the number of hydrocarbon units (-CH$_2$-) in the molecule. Because most tissues contain highly active pyrophosphatase enzymes [21a], which catalyze the virtually irreversible hydrolysis of inorganic pyrophosphate (PP$_i$) to two molecules of inorganic phosphate (P$_i$), reaction [21] proceeds overwhelmingly to completion (i.e., from left to right).

Step 21a

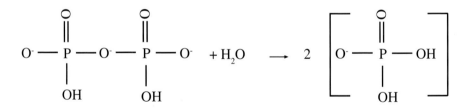

Although fatty acids are activated in this way, the acyl coenzyme A derivatives that are formed must be transported to the enzyme complex that effects their oxidation. Activation occurs in the cytoplasm, but, in animal cells, oxidation takes place in the mitochondria. The transfer of fatty acyl coenzyme A across the mitochondrial membrane is effected by the enzyme carnitine, a nitrogen-containing small hydroxy acid of the formula $(CH_3)_3NCH_2CH(OH)CH_2COO-$.

Step 21b

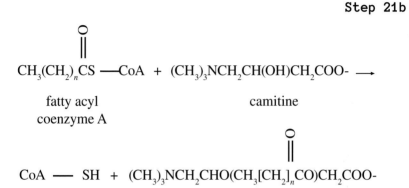

$$CH_3(CH_2)_nCS\!-\!\!-CoA \ + \ (CH_3)_3NCH_2CH(OH)CH_2COO- \longrightarrow$$

fatty acyl   camitine
coenzyme A

$$CoA \!-\!\!- SH \ + \ (CH_3)_3NCH_2CHO(CH_3[CH_2]_nCO)CH_2COO-$$

The -OH group within the carnitine molecule accepts the acyl group of fatty acyl coenzyme A, forming acyl carnitine, which can cross the inner membrane of the mitochondrion and there return the acyl group to coenzyme A.

Step 21c

$$CH_3(CH_2)_nCOOH \ + \ ATP \longrightarrow CH_3(CH_2)_nCOO\circledP \ + \ ADP$$

fatty acid   fatty acyl
phosphate

These reactions are catalyzed by the enzyme carnitine acyl transferase. Defects in this enzyme or in the carnitine carrier are inborn errors of metabolism. In obligate anaerobic bacteria the linkage of fatty acids to coenzyme A may require the formation of a fatty acyl phosphate, in which the phosphorylation of the fatty acid uses ATP. ADP is also a product [21c]. The fatty acyl moiety $[CH_3 (CH_2)_n COO^-]$ is then transferred to coenzyme A [21d], forming a fatty acyl coenzyme A compound and P_i.

Step 21d

$$CH_3(CH_2)_n COO^\circledP + CoA — SH \longrightarrow$$

$$\overset{\overset{\textstyle O}{\|}}{CH_3(CH_2)_n CS} — CoA + P_i$$

fatty acyl
coenzyme A

Initially, as shown in step [22], two hydrogen atoms are lost from the fatty acyl coenzyme A, resulting in the formation of an unsaturated fatty acyl coenzyme A (i.e., with a double bond, -CH=CH-) between the α- and β-carbons of the acyl moiety.

Step 22

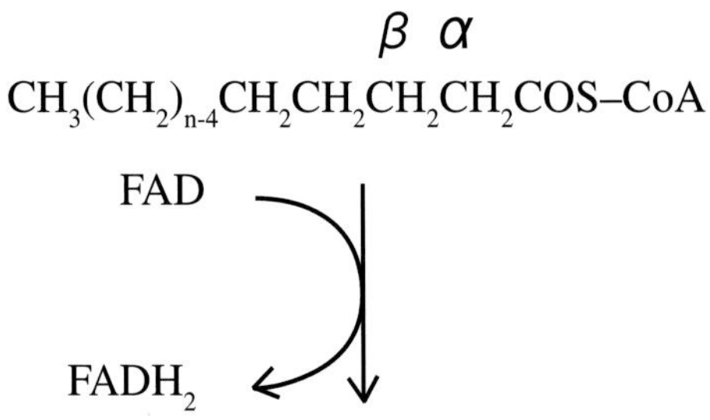

$$\overset{\beta \quad \alpha}{CH_3(CH_2)_{n-4}CH_2CH_2CH_2CH_2COS–CoA}$$

FAD

FADH$_2$

124

$CH_3(CH_2)_{n-4}CH_2CH_2CH = CHCOS\text{--}CoA$

H_2O **Step 23**

OH
|
$CH_3(CH_2)_{n-4}CH_2CH_2CH\ CH_2COS\text{--}CoA$

NAD^+

Step 24

$NADH + H^+$

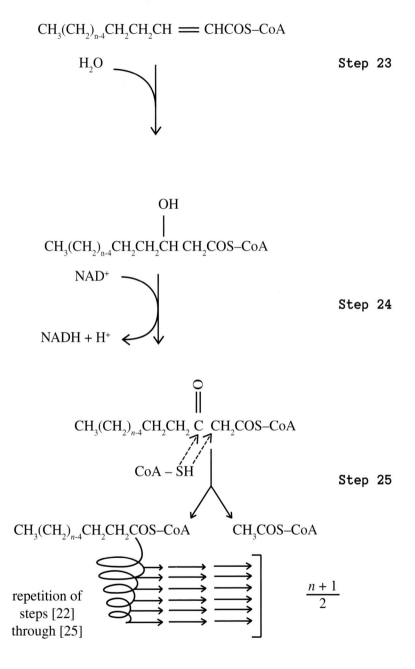

$CH_3(CH_2)_{n-4}CH_2CH_2\ \overset{\overset{O}{\|}}{C}\ CH_2COS\text{--}CoA$

$CoA - SH$ **Step 25**

$CH_3(CH_2)_{n-4}CH_2CH_2COS\text{--}CoA$ $CH_3COS\text{--}CoA$

repetition of
steps [22]
through [25]

$\dfrac{n+1}{2}$

(The α-carbon is the one closest to the carboxyl [-COOH] group of a fatty acid; the next closest is the β-, and so on to the end of the hydrocarbon chain.) The hydrogen atoms are accepted by the coenzyme FAD (flavin adenine dinucleotide), which is reduced to $FADH_2$. The product of step [22], α,β-unsaturated fatty acyl coenzyme A, is enzymatically hydrated [23]—water is added across the double bond. The product, called a β-hydroxyacyl coenzyme A, can again be oxidized in an enzyme-catalyzed reaction [24]. The electrons removed are accepted by NAD^+. The product is called a β-ketoacyl coenzyme A.

The next enzymatic step [25] enables the energy invested in step [21] to be conserved.The β-ketoacyl coenzyme A that is the product of reaction [24] is split, not by water but by coenzyme A. The process, called thiolysis (as distinct from hydrolysis), yields the two-carbon fragment acetyl coenzyme A and a fatty acyl coenzyme A having two fewer carbon atoms than the molecule that underwent reaction [22]. The two compounds are otherwise similar.

The shortened fatty acyl coenzyme A molecule now undergoes the sequence of reactions again, beginning with the dehydrogenation step [22], and another two-carbon fragment is removed as acetyl coenzyme A. With each passage through the process of fatty acid oxidation, the fatty acid loses a two-carbon fragment as acetyl coenzyme A and two pairs of hydrogen atoms to specific acceptors.

The 16-carbon fatty acid, palmitic acid, for example, undergoes a total of seven such cycles, yielding eight molecules of acetyl coenzyme A and 14 pairs of hydrogen atoms, seven of which appear in the form of $FADH_2$ and seven in the form of $NADH + H^+$. The reduced coenzymes, $FADH_2$ and reduced NAD^+, are reoxidized when the electrons pass through the electron transport chain, with concomitant formation of ATP. In anaerobes, organic molecules and not oxygen are electron acceptors. Thus, the yield of ATP is reduced. In all organisms, however, the acetyl coenzyme A formed from the breakdown of fatty acids joins that arising from the catabolism of carbohydrates and many amino acids.

Fatty acids with an odd number of carbon atoms are relatively rare in nature but may arise during microbial fermentations or through the oxidation of amino acids such as valine and isoleucine. They may be fragmented through repeated cycles of steps [22] to [25] until the final five-carbon acyl coenzyme A is split into acetyl coenzyme A and propionyl coenzyme A, which has three carbon atoms. In many bacteria this propionyl coenzyme A can be transformed either to acetyl coenzyme A and carbon dioxide or to pyruvate. In other microorganisms and in animals propionyl coenzyme A has a different fate: carbon dioxide is added to propionyl coenzyme A in a reaction requiring ATP. The product, methylmalonyl coenzyme A, has four carbon atoms. The molecule undergoes a rearrangement, forming succinyl coenzyme A, which is an intermediate of the TCA cycle.

CATABOLISM OF PROTEINS

The amino acids derived from proteins function primarily as the precursors, or building blocks, for the cell's own proteins and (unlike lipids and carbohydrates) are not primarily a source of energy. Many microorganisms, on the other hand, can grow by using amino acids as the sole carbon and nitrogen source. Under these conditions these microorganisms derive from the amino acids all of their required energy and all of the precursors of the macromolecules that comprise the components of their cells. Moreover, it has been calculated that a male human of average weight (70 kg [154 pounds]) turns over about 0.4 kg (0.88 lbs) of protein per day. About 0.1 kg (.22 lbs) is degraded and replaced by dietary amino acids, and the remaining 0.3 kg (.66 lbs) is recycled as part of the dynamic state of cell constituents. The cells of plants contain and metabolize many amino acids in addition to the 20 or so that are normally found in proteins.

Before proteins can enter cells, the bonds linking adjacent amino acids (peptide bonds) must be hydrolyzed. This process releases the amino acids constituting the protein. The utilization of dietary proteins thus requires the operation of extracellular digestive enzymes—enzymes outside the cell. Many microorganisms secrete such enzymes into the nutrient media in which they are growing, and animals secrete them into the gut. The turnover of proteins within cells, on the other hand, requires the functioning of intracellular enzymes that catalyze the splitting of the peptide bonds linking adjacent amino acids.

Amino acids may be described by the general formula $RCH(NH_2)COOH$, or $RCH(NH_3^+)COO^-$, in which R represents a specific chemical moiety. The catabolic fate of amino acids involves (1) removal of nitrogen, (2) disposal of nitrogen, and (3) oxidation of the remaining carbon skeleton.

REMOVAL OF NITROGEN

The removal of the amino group ($-NH_2$) generally constitutes the first stage in amino-acid catabolism. The amino group usually is initially transferred to the anion of one of three different α-keto acids (i.e., of the general structure $RCOCOO^-$): pyruvate, which is an intermediate of carbohydrate fragmentation; or oxaloacetate or α-oxoglutarate, both intermediates of the TCA cycle. The products are alanine, aspartate, and glutamate (reactions [26a, b, and c]).

Step 26a

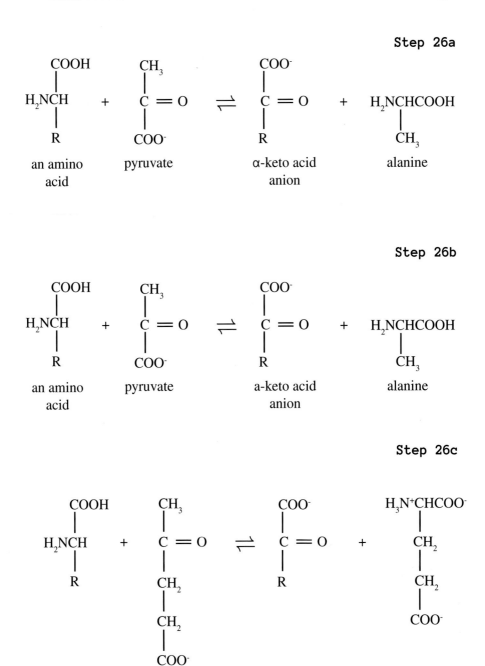

COOH	CH$_3$	COO$^-$	
H$_2$NCH +	C = O ⇌	C = O +	H$_2$NCHCOOH
R	COO$^-$	R	CH$_3$
an amino acid	pyruvate	α-keto acid anion	alanine

Step 26b

COOH	CH$_3$	COO$^-$	
H$_2$NCH +	C = O ⇌	C = O +	H$_2$NCHCOOH
R	COO$^-$	R	CH$_3$
an amino acid	pyruvate	a-keto acid anion	alanine

Step 26c

COOH	CH$_3$	COO$^-$	H$_3$N$^+$CHCOO$^-$
H$_2$NCH +	C = O ⇌	C = O +	CH$_2$
R	CH$_2$	R	CH$_2$
	CH$_2$		COO$^-$
	COO$^-$		
an amino acid	α-oxoglutarate	α-keto acid anion	glutamate

130

Since the effect of these reactions is to produce n amino acids and n keto acids from n different amino acids and n different keto acids, no net reduction in the nitrogen content of the system has yet been achieved. The elimination of nitrogen occurs in a variety of ways.

In many microorganisms, ammonia (NH_3) can be removed from aspartate via a reaction catalyzed by aspartase [27]. The other product, fumarate, is an intermediate of the TCA cycle.

Step 27

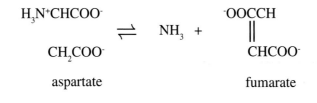

aspartate   fumarate

A quantitatively more important route is that catalyzed by glutamate dehydrogenase, in which the glutamate formed in [26c] is oxidized to α-oxoglutarate, another TCA cycle intermediate [28]. Either $NADP^+$ or both $NADP^+$ and NAD^+ may serve as the hydrogen or electron acceptor, depending on the organism. Some organisms synthesize two enzymes, one of which prefers $NADP^+$ and the other NAD^+. In reaction [28], $NAD(P)^+$ is used to indicate that either NAD^+, $NADP^+$, or both may serve as the electron acceptor.

The occurrence of the transfer reactions [26] and either step [27] or, more importantly, step [28] allows the channeling of many amino acids into a common pathway by which nitrogen can be eliminated as ammonia.

Step 28

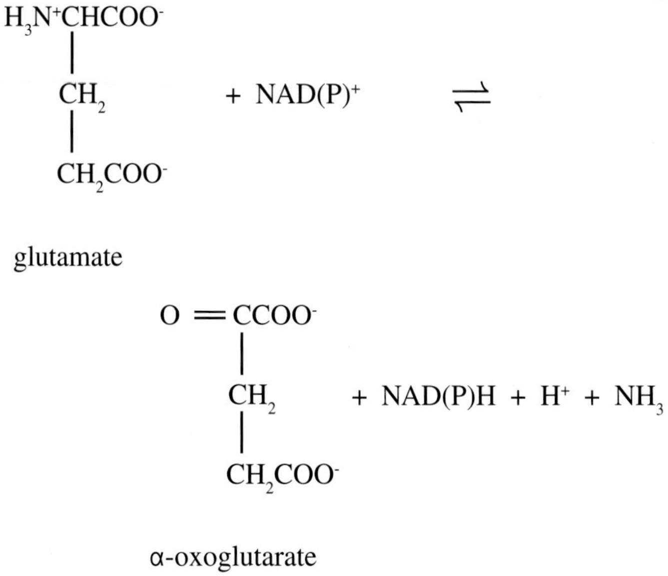

$H_3N^+CHCOO^-$
|
CH_2 $+ NAD(P)^+$ $\rightleftharpoons$
|
CH_2COO^-

glutamate

$O = CCOO^-$
|
CH_2 $+ NAD(P)H + H^+ + NH_3$
|
CH_2COO^-

α-oxoglutarate

DISPOSAL OF NITROGEN

In animals that excrete ammonia as the main nitrogenous waste product (e.g., some marine invertebrates, crustaceans), it is derived from nitrogen transfer reactions [26] and oxidation via glutamate dehydrogenase [28].

Because ammonia is toxic to cells, however, it is detoxified as it forms. This process involves an enzyme-catalyzed reaction between ammonia and a molecule of glutamate. ATP provides the energy for the reaction, which results in the formation of glutamine, ADP, and inorganic phosphate [29]. This reaction [29] is catalyzed by glutamine synthetase, which is subject to a variety of metabolic controls. The glutamine thus formed gives up the amide nitrogen in the kidney tubules. As a result glutamate is formed once again, and ammonia is released into the urine.

Step 29

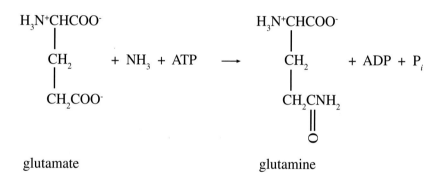

glutamate   glutamine

In terrestrial reptiles and birds, uric acid rather than glutamate is the compound with which nitrogen combines to form a nontoxic substance for transfer to the kidney tubules. Uric acid is formed by a complex pathway that begins with ribose 5-phosphate and during which a so-called purine skeleton is formed. In the course of this process, nitrogen atoms from glutamine and the amino acids aspartic acid and glycine are

133

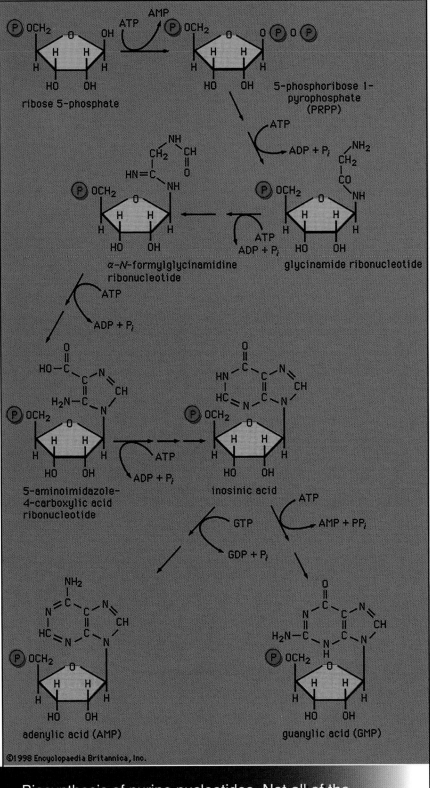

Biosynthesis of purine nucleotides. Not all of the intermediate compounds formed are shown.

incorporated into the skeleton. These nitrogen donors are derived from other amino acids via amino group transfer [26] and the reaction catalyzed by glutamine synthetase [29].

In most fishes, amphibians, and mammals, nitrogen is detoxified in the liver and excreted as urea, a readily soluble and harmless product. The sequence leading to the formation of urea, commonly called the urea cycle, is summarized as follows: Ammonia, formed from glutamate and NAD^+ in the liver mitochondria (reaction [28]), reacts with carbon dioxide and ATP to form carbamoyl phosphate, ADP, and inorganic phosphate, as shown in reaction [30].

Step 30

$$NH_3 + CO_2 + 2ATP \longrightarrow \underset{\substack{\text{carbamoyl} \\ \text{phosphate}}}{NH_2COO®} + 2ADP + P_i$$

The reaction is catalyzed by carbamoyl phosphate synthetase. The carbamoyl moiety of carbamoyl phosphate (NH_2CO-) is transferred to ornithine, an amino acid, in a reaction catalyzed by ornithine transcarbamoylase. The products of this reaction are citrulline and inorganic phosphate [31]. Citrulline and aspartate formed from amino acids via step [26b] react to form argininosuccinate [32]. Argininosuccinic acid synthetase catalyzes the reaction. Argininosuccinate splits into fumarate and arginine during a reaction catalyzed by argininosuccinase [32a].

Step 31

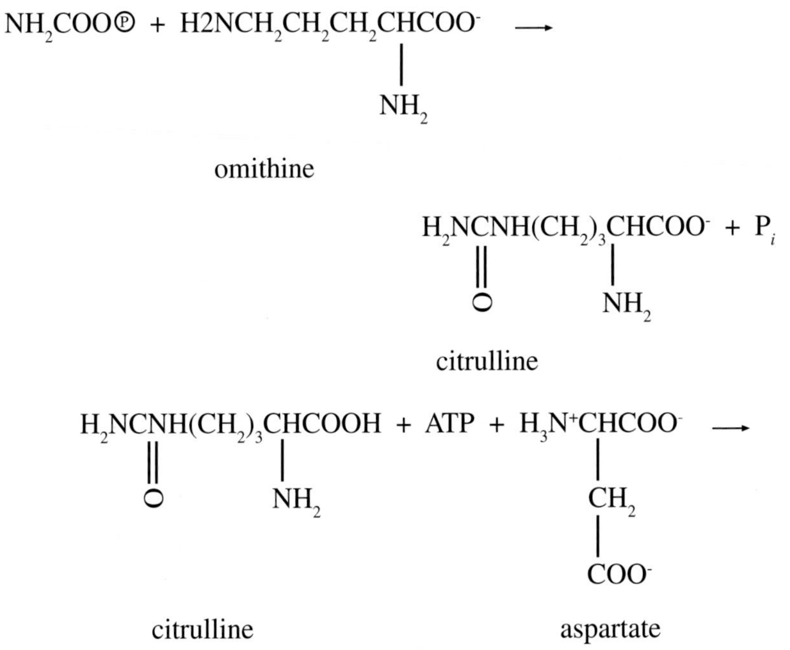

$$NH_2COO^{℗} + H2NCH_2CH_2CH_2CHCOO^- \longrightarrow$$
$$\phantom{NH_2COO^{℗} + H2NCH_2CH_2CH_2CHC}|$$
$$\phantom{NH_2COO^{℗} + H2NCH_2CH_2CH_2C}NH_2$$

omithine

$$H_2NCNH(CH_2)_3CHCOO^- + P_i$$
$$\| |$$
$$O NH_2$$

citrulline

$$H_2NCNH(CH_2)_3CHCOOH + ATP + H_3N^+CHCOO^- \longrightarrow$$
$$\| ||$$
$$O NH_2 CH_2$$
$$|$$
$$COO^-$$

citrulline   aspartate

Step 32

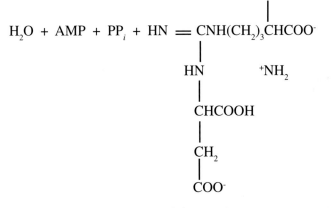

$$H_2O + AMP + PP_i + HN = CNH(CH_2)_3CHCOO^-$$

with substituents:

HN $^+NH_2$

CHCOOH

CH_2

COO^-

argininosuccinate

Step 32a

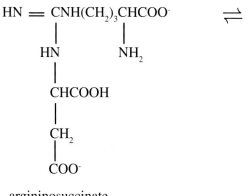

argininosuccinate

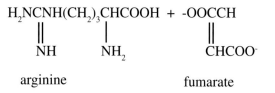

arginine   fumarate

In the final step of the urea cycle, arginine, in a reaction catalyzed by arginase, is hydrolyzed [33]. Urea and ornithine are the products. Ornithine thus is available to initiate another cycle beginning at step [31].

Step 33

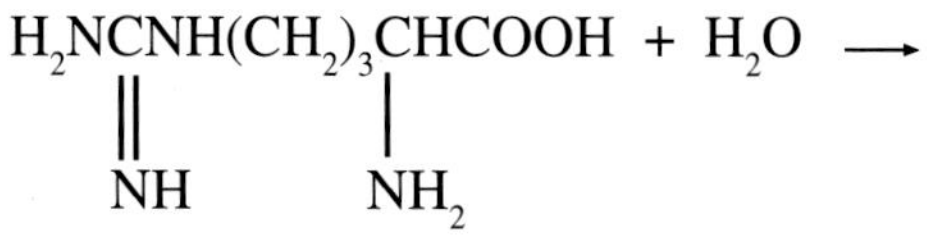

$$H_2NCNH(CH_2)_3CHCOOH + H_2O \longrightarrow$$

NH   NH$_2$

arginine

137

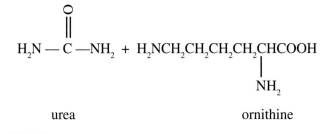

$$H_2N-C-NH_2 + H_2NCH_2CH_2CH_2CH_2CHCOOH$$

urea   ornithine

OXIDATION OF THE CARBON SKELETON

The carbon skeletons of amino acids (i.e., the portion of the molecule remaining after the removal of nitrogen) are fragmented to form only a few end products, all of which are intermediates of either glycolysis or the TCA cycle. The number and complexity of the catabolic steps by which each amino acid arrives at its catabolic end point reflects the chemical complexity of that amino acid. Thus, in the case of alanine, only the amino group must be removed to yield pyruvate. The amino acid threonine, on the other hand, must be transformed successively to the amino acids glycine and serine before pyruvate is formed. The fragmentation of leucine to acetyl coenzyme A involves seven steps, and that of tryptophan to the same end product requires 11.

CHAPTER

4

THE COMBUSTION OF FOOD MATERIALS

Although the pathways for fragmentation of food materials effect the conversion of a large variety of relatively complex starting materials into only a few simpler intermediates of central metabolic routes—mainly pyruvate, acetyl coenzyme A, and a few intermediates of the TCA cycle—their operation releases but a fraction of the energy contained in the materials. The reason is that, in the fermentation process, catabolic intermediates serve also as the terminal acceptors of the reducing equivalents (hydrogen atoms or electrons) that are removed during the oxidation of food. The end products thus may be at the same oxidation level and may contain equivalent numbers of carbon, hydrogen, and oxygen atoms, as the material that was catabolized by a fermentative route. The necessity for pyruvate, for example, to act as hydrogen acceptor in the fermentation of glucose to lactate results in the conservation of all the component atoms of the glucose molecule in the form of lactate. The consequent release of energy as ATP is thus small.

A more favourable situation arises if the reducing equivalents formed by oxidation of nutrients can be passed on to an inorganic acceptor such as oxygen. In this case, the products of fermentation need not act as "hydrogen sinks," in which the energy in the molecule is lost when they leave the cell. Instead, the products of fermentation can be degraded further, during phase III of catabolism, and all the usable chemical energy of the nutrient can be transformed into ATP.

OXIDATION OF MOLECULAR FRAGMENTS

Oxidation entails the loss of electrons from a reacting fragment and is fundamental to the process of cellular respiration. Pyruvate, formed from glycolysis in the cytoplasm of eukaryotic cells, is transported into mitochondria, where it undergoes oxidation, thereby generating acetyl coenzyme A. Acetyl coenzyme A is used to fuel the TCA cycle, which produces NADH + H^+ reducing equivalents that enter the electron transport chain in the inner mitochondrial membrane. In addition to pyruvate, other molecular fragments susceptible to oxidation include fats and amino acids.

OXIDATION OF PYRUVATE

The oxidation of pyruvate involves the concerted action of several enzymes and coenzymes collectively called the pyruvate dehydrogenase complex—a multienzyme complex in which the substrates are passed consecutively from one enzyme to the next, and the product of the reaction catalyzed by the first enzyme immediately becomes the substrate for the second enzyme in the complex. The overall reaction is the formation of acetyl coenzyme A and carbon dioxide from pyruvate, with concomitant liberation of two reducing equivalents in the form of NADH + H+. The individual reactions that result in the formation of these end products are as follows.

Pyruvate first reacts with the coenzyme of pyruvic acid decarboxylase (enzyme 1), thiamine pyrophosphate (TPP). In addition to carbon dioxide a hydroxyethyl–TPP–enzyme complex ("active acetaldehyde") is formed [1]. Thiamine is vitamin B$_1$, and the biological role of TPP was first revealed by the inability of vitamin B$_1$-deficient animals to oxidize pyruvate.

Step 1

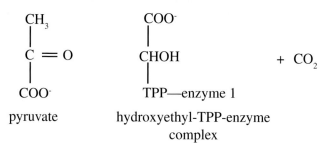

pyruvate   hydroxyethyl-TPP-enzyme
complex

The hydroxyethyl moiety formed in [1] is immediately transferred to one of the two sulfur atoms (S) of the coenzyme (6,8-dithio-*n*-octanoateor lipS$_2$) of the second enzyme in the complex, dihydrolipoyl transacetylase (enzyme 2). The hydroxyethyl group attaches to lipS$_2$ at one of its sulfur atoms, as shown in [2]. The result is that coenzyme lipS$_2$ is reduced and the hydroxyethyl moiety is oxidized.

Step 2

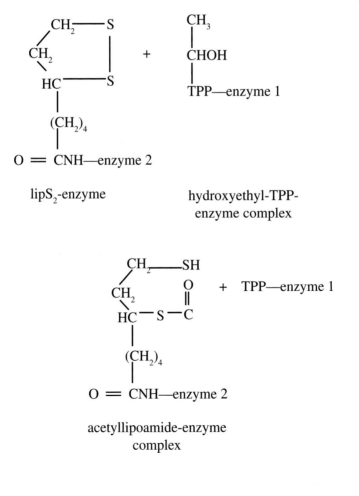

lipS$_2$-enzyme

hydroxyethyl-TPP-enzyme complex

acetyllipoamide-enzyme complex

The acetyl group then is transferred to the sulfhy-dryl (-SH) group of coenzyme A, thereby completing the oxidation of pyruvate (reaction [3]). The coenzyme $lipS_2$ that accepted the hydroxyethyl moiety in step [2] of the sequence, now reduced, must be reoxidized before another molecule of pyruvate can be oxi-dized. The reoxidation of the coenzyme is achieved by the enzyme-catalyzed transfer of two reducing equivalents initially to the coenzyme flavin adenine dinucleotide (FAD) and thence to the NAD^+ that is the first carrier in the so-called electron transport chain. The passage of two such reducing equivalents from reduced NAD^+ to oxygen is accompanied by the for-mation of three molecules of ATP.

Step 3

$$CH_2 \text{—} SH$$
$$CH_2$$
$$HC \text{——} C \overset{O}{\underset{\|}{}} \quad + \quad CoA\text{—}SH \quad \longrightarrow$$
$$(CH_2)_4$$
$$O = CNH\text{—enzyme 2} \qquad \text{coenzyme A}$$

$$CH_3CS\text{—CoA} \overset{O}{\underset{\|}{}} \quad + \quad CH_2 \text{—} SH$$
$$CH_2$$
$$HC \text{——} SH$$
$$(CH_2)_4$$
$$O = CNH\text{—enzyme 2}$$

acetyl coenzyme A

$lip(SH)_2$-enzyme

143

The overall reaction may be written as shown in [4], in which pyruvate reacts with coenzyme A in the presence of TPP and $lipS_2$ to form acetyl coenzyme A and carbon dioxide, and to liberate two hydrogen atoms (in the form of NADH + H$^+$) that can subsequently yield energy by the reduction of oxygen to water. The $lipS_2$ reduced during this process is reoxidized in the presence of the enzyme lipoyl dehydrogenase, with the concomitant reduction of NAD$^+$.

Step 4

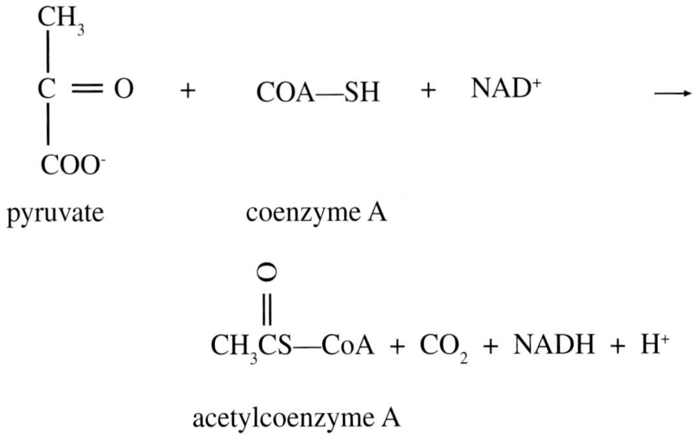

$$\begin{array}{c} CH_3 \\ | \\ C = O \\ | \\ COO^- \end{array} \quad + \quad COA-SH \quad + \quad NAD^+ \quad \longrightarrow$$

pyruvate $\qquad$ coenzyme A

$$\overset{\overset{\textstyle O}{\|}}{CH_3CS}-CoA + CO_2 + NADH + H^+$$

acetylcoenzyme A

THE TCA CYCLE

Acetyl coenzyme A arises not only from the oxidation of pyruvate but also from that of fats and many of the amino acids comprising proteins. The sequence of enzyme-catalyzed steps that effects the total combustion of the acetyl moiety of the coenzyme represents the terminal oxidative pathway for virtually all food materials. The balance of the overall reaction of the TCA cycle [4a] is that three molecules of water react with acetyl coenzyme A to form carbon dioxide, coenzyme A, and reducing equivalents. The oxidation by oxygen of the reducing equivalents is accompanied by the conservation (as ATP) of most of the energy of the food ingested by aerobic organisms.

Step 4a

$$CH_3CS{-}CoA + 3H_2O \quad 2CO_2 + CoA{-}SH + 4[2H]$$

acetylcoenzyme A   reducing
                                                             equivalents

FORMATION OF COENZYME A, CARBON DIOXIDE, AND REDUCING EQUIVALENT

The relative complexity and number of chemical events that constitute the TCA cycle, and their location as components of spatially determined structures such as cell membranes in microorganisms and mitochondria in plants and higher animals, reflect the problems involved chemically in "dismembering" a compound having only two carbon atoms and releasing in a controlled and stepwise manner the reducing equivalents ultimately to be passed to oxygen. These problems have been overcome by the simple but effective device of initially combining the two-carbon compound with a four-carbon acceptor. It is much less difficult chemically to dismember and oxidize a compound having six carbon atoms.

Step 5

$$CH_3CS-CoA \quad + \quad CCOO^- \quad + \quad H_2O \quad \longrightarrow \quad HOCCOO^- \quad + \quad CoA-SH$$

acetyl coenzyme A   oxaloacetate   citrate

In the TCA cycle, acetyl coenzyme A initially reacts with oxaloacetate to yield citrate and to liberate coenzyme A. This reaction [5] is catalyzed by citrate synthase. Citrate undergoes isomerization (i.e., a rear-rangement of certain atoms comprising the molecule) to form isocitrate [6]. The reaction involves first the removal of the elements of water from citrate to form cis-aconitate, and then the re-addition of water to cis-aconitate in such a way that isocitrate is formed. It is probable that all three reactants—citrate, cis-aconitate, and isocitrate—remain closely associated with aconitase, the enzyme that catalyzes the isomeriza-tion process, and that most of the cis-aconitate is not

146

released from the enzyme surface but is immediately converted to isocitrate.

Step 6

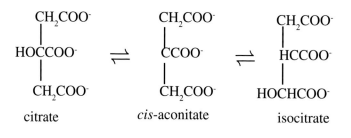

$$\underset{\text{citrate}}{\begin{array}{c} CH_2COO^- \\ | \\ HOCCOO^- \\ | \\ CH_2COO^- \end{array}} \rightleftharpoons \underset{\text{cis-aconitate}}{\begin{array}{c} CH_2COO^- \\ | \\ CCOO^- \\ || \\ CH_2COO^- \end{array}} \rightleftharpoons \underset{\text{isocitrate}}{\begin{array}{c} CH_2COO^- \\ | \\ HCCOO^- \\ | \\ HOCHCOO^- \end{array}}$$

Isocitrate is oxidized—i.e., hydrogen is removed—to form oxalosuccinate. The two hydrogen atoms are usually transferred to NAD⁺, thus forming reduced NAD⁺ [7].

Step 7

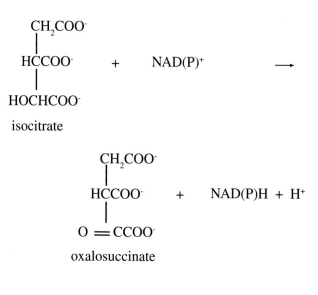

$$\underset{\text{isocitrate}}{\begin{array}{c} CH_2COO^- \\ | \\ HCCOO^- \\ | \\ HOCHCOO^- \end{array}} + NAD(P)^+ \longrightarrow$$

$$\underset{\text{oxalosuccinate}}{\begin{array}{c} CH_2COO^- \\ | \\ HCCOO^- \\ | \\ O = CCOO^- \end{array}} + NAD(P)H + H^+$$

147

In some microorganisms, and during the biosynthesis of glutamate in the cytoplasm of animal cells, however, the hydrogen atoms may also be accepted by NADP+. Thus the enzyme controlling this reaction, isocitrate dehydrogenase, differs in specificity for the coenzymes. Various forms occur not only in different organisms but even within the same cell. In [7] NAD(P)+ indicates that either NAD' or NADP+ can act as a hydrogen acceptor.

The position of the carboxylate (-COO⁻) that is "sandwiched" in the middle of the oxalosuccinate molecule renders it very unstable. As a result, the carbon of this group is lost as carbon dioxide (note the dotted rectangle) in a reaction [8] that can occur spontaneously but may be further accelerated by an enzyme.

Step 8

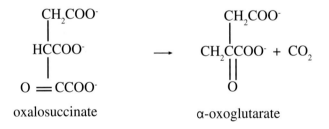

oxalosuccinate   α-oxoglutarate

The five-carbon product of reaction [8], α-oxoglutarate, has chemical properties similar to pyruvate (free-acid forms of both are so-called α-oxoacids), and the chemical events involved in the oxidation of α-oxoglutarate are analogous to those already described

148

for the oxidation of pyruvate (see reaction [4]). Reaction [9] is effected by a multi-enzyme complex. TPP, $lipS_2$ (6,8-dithio-n-octanoate), and coenzyme A are required as coenzymes. The products are carbon dioxide and succinyl coenzyme A. As was noted with reaction [4], this oxidation of α-oxoglutarate results in the reduction of $lipS_2$, which must be reoxidized. This is done by transfer of reducing equivalents to FAD and thence to NAD^+. The resultant $NADH + H^+$ is reoxidized by the passage of the electrons, ultimately, to oxygen, via the electron transport chain.

Step 9

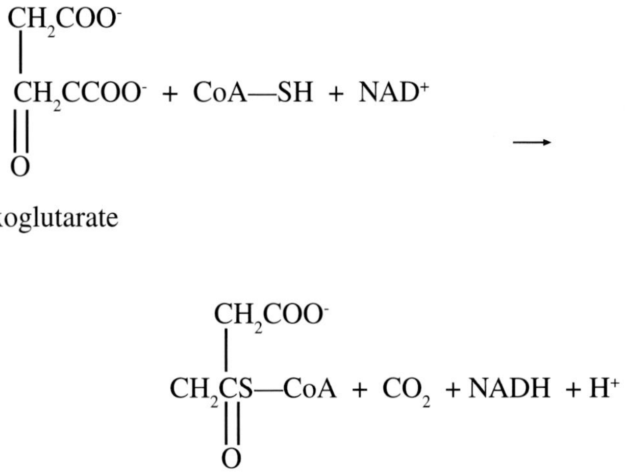

$$CH_2COO^-$$
$$|$$
$$CH_2CCOO^- + CoA{-}SH + NAD^+ \longrightarrow$$
$$||$$
$$O$$

α-oxoglutarate

$$CH_2COO^-$$
$$|$$
$$CH_2CS{-}CoA + CO_2 + NADH + H^+$$
$$||$$
$$O$$

succinyl
coenzyme A

Unlike the acetyl coenzyme A produced from pyruvate in reaction [4], succinyl coenzyme A undergoes a phosphorolysis reaction—i.e., transfer of the succinyl moiety from coenzyme A to inorganic phosphate. The succinyl phosphate thus formed is not released from the enzyme surface. Rather, as an unstable, high-energy compound called an acid anhydride, it transfers a high-energy phosphate to ADP, directly or via guanosine diphosphate (GDP) [10].

Step 10

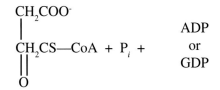

succinyl
coenzyme A

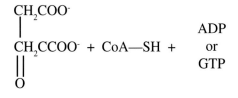

succinate

If guanosine triphosphate (GTP) forms, ATP can readily arise from it in an exchange involving ADP [10a]:

$$GTP + ADP \rightleftharpoons ATP + GDP$$

Step 10a

ISOMERIZATION

Isomerization is the chemical process by which a compound is transformed into any of its isomeric forms—forms with the same chemical composition but with different structure or configuration and, hence, generally with different physical and chemical properties. An example is the conversion of butane, a hydrocarbon with four carbon atoms joined in a straight chain, to its branched-chain isomer, isobutane, by heating the butane to 100 °C (212 °F) or higher in the presence of a catalyst. Butane and isobutane have widely different properties. Butane boils at -0.5 °C (31.1 °F) and freezes at -138.3 °C (-216.9 °F), whereas isobutane boils at -11.7 °C (10.9 °F) and freezes at -159.6 °C (-255.3 °F). More important from the commercial standpoint, branched-chain hydrocarbons are better motor fuels than their straight-chain isomers. The isomerization of straight-chain hydrocarbons to their corresponding branched-chain isomers is an important step (called reforming) in gasoline manufacture. There are numerous other examples of isomerization reactions of great industrial importance.

REGENERATION OF OXALOACETATE

The remainder of the reactions of the TCA cycle serve to regenerate the initial four-carbon acceptor of acetyl coenzyme A (oxaloacetate) from succinate, the process requiring in effect the oxidation of a methylene group (-CH²-) to a carbonyl group (-CO-), with concomitant release of 2' [2H] reducing equivalents. It is therefore similar to, and is effected in like manner to, the oxidation of fatty acids. As is the case with fatty acids, hydrogen atoms or electrons are initially removed from the succinate formed in [10] and are accepted by FAD. The reaction, catalyzed by succinate dehydrogenase [11], results in the formation of fumarate and reduced FAD.

Step 11

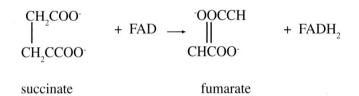

| succinate | | fumarate |

The elements of water are added across the double bond (-CH=CH-) of fumarate in a reaction catalyzed by fumarase [12]. This type of reaction also occurred in step [6] of the cycle. The product of reaction [12] is malate.

Step 12

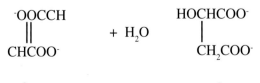

| fumarate | | malate |

Malate can be oxidized to oxaloacetate by removal of two hydrogen atoms, which are accepted by NAD+. This type of reaction, catalyzed by malate dehydrogenase in reaction [13], also occurred in step [7] of the cycle. The formation of oxaloacetate completes the TCA cycle, which can now begin again with the formation of citrate [5].

Step 13

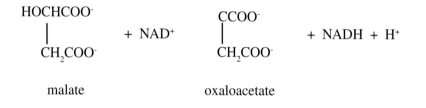

malate   oxaloacetate

ATP Yield of Aerobic Oxidation

The loss of the two molecules of carbon dioxide in steps [8] and [9] does not yield biologically useful energy. The substrate-linked formation of ATP accompanies step [10], in which one molecule of ATP is formed during each turn of the cycle. The hydrogen ions and electrons that result from steps [7], [9], [11], and [13] are passed down the chain of respiratory carriers to oxygen, with the concomitant formation of three molecules of ATP, per [2H], as NADH + H+. Similarly, the oxidation

153

of the reduced FAD formed in [11] results in the formation of two ATP. Each turn of the cycle thus leads to the production of a total of 12 ATP. It will be recalled that the anaerobic fragmentation of glucose to two molecules of pyruvate yielded two ATP. The aerobic oxidation via the TCA cycle of two molecules of pyruvate thus makes available to the cell at least 15 times more ATP per molecule of glucose catabolized than is produced anaerobically. If, in addition, the $2 \times$ [NADH + H^+] generated per glucose in the oxidation of glyceraldehyde 3-phosphate are passed on to oxygen, a further six ATP are generated. The advantage to living organisms is to be able to respire rather than merely to ferment.

BIOLOGICAL ENERGY TRANSDUCTION

Energy transduction is the passage of energy from an electron donor to an electron acceptor. In cells, energy transduction is used to generate ATP via the electron transport chain, in which electrons are transferred from NADH (an electron donor) to oxygen (an electron acceptor). Oxygen then combines with protons to form water. Electron transport, which takes place in the inner membrane of mitochondria, results in the movement of protons into the intermembrane space (the space between the inner and outer mitochondrial membranes), thereby establishing a proton gradient across the mitochondrial membrane. This gradient generates the potential necessary for the phosphorylation of ADP to ATP.

The electron transport chain generates the majority of cellular ATP, which releases large amounts of free energy when it phosphorylates substances in cells. Free energy is the maximum amount of work that can be obtained from a reaction, and it is an important component of the energy-releasing processes in living organisms.

ATP AS THE CURRENCY OF ENERGY EXCHANGE

When the terminal phosphate group is removed from ATP by hydrolysis, two negatively charged products are formed, ADP^{3-} and HPO_4^{2-} (a phosphate group) [14].

Step 14

$$ATP^{4-} + H_2O \longrightarrow ADP_3^- + HPO_4^{2-} + H^+$$

These products are electrically more stable than the parent molecule and do not readily recombine. The total free energy (G) of the products is much less than that of ATP, and hence energy is liberated (i.e., the reaction is exergonic).

The amount of energy liberated under strictly defined conditions is called the standard free energy change (ΔG′). This value for the hydrolysis of ATP is relatively high, at -8 kilocalories per mole. (One kilocalorie is the amount of heat required to raise the temperature of 1,000 grams of water one degree centigrade.) Conversely, the formation of

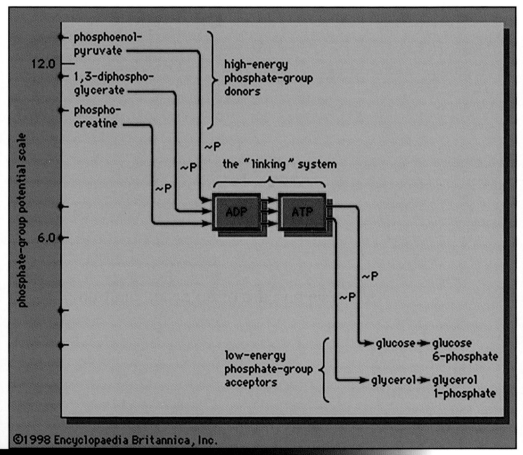

The transfer of phosphate groups from high-energy donors to low-energy acceptors by way of the ATP–ADP system

ATP from ADP and inorganic phosphate (P_i) is an energy-requiring (i.e., endergonic) reaction with a standard free energy change of +8 kilocalories per mole. The hydrolysis of the remaining phosphate-to-phosphate bond of ADP is also accompanied by a liberation of free energy (the standard free energy change is -6.5 kilocalories per mole). AMP hydrolysis liberates less energy (the standard free energy change is -2.2 kilocalories per mole).

The free energy of hydrolysis of a compound thus is a measure of the difference in energy content between the starting substances (reactants) and the final substances (products). ATP does not have the highest standard free energy of hydrolysis of all the naturally occurring phosphates but instead occupies a position at approximately the halfway point in a series of phosphate compounds with a wide range of standard free energies of hydrolysis. Compounds such as 1,3-diphosphoglycerate or phosphoenolpyruvate (PEP), which are above ATP on the scale, have large negative $\Delta G'$ values on hydrolysis and are often called high-energy phosphates. They are said to exhibit a high phosphate group transfer potential because they have a tendency to lose their phosphate groups. Compounds such as glucose 6-phosphate or fructose 6-phosphate, which are below ATP on the scale because they have smaller negative $\Delta G'$ values on hydrolysis, have a tendency to hold on to their phosphate groups and thus act as low-energy phosphate acceptors.

Both ATP and ADP act as intermediate carriers for the transfer of phosphate groups (which are more precisely called phosphoryl groups) and hence of energy, from compounds lying above ATP to those lying beneath it. Thus, in glycolysis, ADP acts as an acceptor of a phosphate group during the synthesis of ATP from PEP, and ATP functions as a donor of a phosphate group during the formation of fructose 1,6-diphosphate from fructose 6-phosphate.

The first step in glycolysis, the formation of glucose 6-phosphate (G6P), illustrates how an energetically unfavourable reaction may become feasible under intracellular conditions by coupling it to ATP.

glucose + P_i ⟶ G6P　　　　　　$\Delta G'$ = +3.3 kcal **Step 15**

ATP ⟶ ADP + P_i　　　　　　　$\Delta G'$ = -7.3 kcal **Step 15a**

glucose + ATP ⟶ G6P + ADP　　$\Delta G'$ = -4 kcal **Step 15b**

ATP ⟶ ADP + P_i　　　　　　　$\Delta G'$ = -7.3 kcal **Step 15a**

glucose + ATP ⟶ G6P + ADP　　$\Delta G'$ = -4 kcal **Step 15b**

Reaction [15] has a positive $\Delta G'$ value, indicating that the reaction tends to proceed in the reverse direction. It is therefore necessary to use the standard free energy generated by the breaking

158

of the first phosphate bond in ATP (reaction [15a]), which is -7.3 kilocalories per mole, to move reaction [15] in the forward direction. Combining these reactions and their standard free energies gives reaction [15b] and a standard free energy value of -4 kilocalories per mole, indicating that the reaction will proceed in the forward direction. There are many intracellular reactions in which the formation of ADP or AMP from ATP provides energy for otherwise unfavourable biosyntheses. Some cellular reactions use equivalent phosphorylated analogues of ATP, for example, guanosine triphosphate (GTP) for protein synthesis.

In certain specialized cells or tissues the chemical energy of ATP is used to perform work other than the chemical work of anabolism. One example is mechanical work—such as muscular contraction, or the movement of contractile structures called cilia and flagella, which are responsible for the motility of many small organisms. The performance of osmotic work also requires ATP. An example of this form of work is the transport of ions or metabolites through membranes against a concentration gradient, a process that is basically responsible for many physiological functions, including nerve conduction, the secretion of hydrochloric acid in the stomach, and the removal of water from the kidneys.

FREE ENERGY

In thermodynamics, free energy is an energy-like property or state function of a system in thermodynamic equilibrium. Free energy has the dimensions of energy, and its value is determined by the state of the system and not by its history. Free energy is used to determine how systems change and how much work they can produce. It is expressed in two forms: the Helmholtz free energy F, sometimes called the work function, and the Gibbs free energy G. If U is the internal energy of a system, PV the pressure-volume product, and TS the temperature-entropy product (T being the temperature above absolute zero), then $F = U - TS$ and $G = U + PV - TS$. The latter equation can also be written in the form $G = H - TS$, where $H = U + PV$ is the enthalpy. Free energy is an extensive property, meaning that its magnitude depends on the amount of a substance in a given thermodynamic state.

The changes in free energy, ΔF or ΔG, are useful in determining the direction of spontaneous change and evaluating the maximum work that can be obtained from thermodynamic processes involving chemical or other types of reactions. In a reversible process the maximum useful work that can be obtained from a system under constant temperature and constant volume is equal to the (negative) change in the Helmholtz free energy, $-\Delta F = -\Delta U + T\Delta S$, and the maximum useful work under constant temperature and constant pressure (other than work done against the atmosphere) is equal to the (negative) change in the Gibbs free energy, $-\Delta G = -\Delta H + T\Delta S$. In each case, the $T\Delta S$ entropy term represents the heat absorbed by the system from a heat reservoir at temperature T under conditions where the system does maximum work. By conservation of energy, the total work done also includes the decrease in internal energy U or enthalpy H as the case may be. For example, the energy for the maximum electrical work done by a battery as it discharges comes both from the decrease in its internal energy due to chemical reactions and from the heat $T\Delta S$ it absorbs in order to keep its temperature constant, which is the ideal maximum heat that can be absorbed. For any actual battery, the electrical work done would be less than the maximum work, and the heat absorbed would be correspondingly less than $T\Delta S$.

Changes in free energy can be used to judge whether changes of state can occur spontaneously. Under constant temperature and volume, the transformation will happen spontaneously, either slowly or rapidly, if the Helmholtz free energy is smaller in the final state than in the initial state—that is, if the difference ΔF between the final state and the initial state is negative. Under constant temperature and pressure, the transformation of state will occur spontaneously if the change in the Gibbs free energy, ΔG, is negative.

(continued on the next page)

(continued from the previous page)

Phase transitions provide instructive examples, as when ice melts to form water at 0.01°C (T = 273.16 K), with the solid and liquid phases in equilibrium. Then ΔH = 79.71 calories per gram is the latent heat of fusion, and by definition $\Delta S = \Delta H/_T$ = 0.292 calories per gram·K is the entropy change. It follows immediately that $\Delta G = \Delta H - T\Delta S$ is zero, indicating that the two phases are in equilibrium and that no useful work can be extracted from the phase transition (other than work against the atmosphere due to changes in pressure and volume). Furthermore, ΔG is negative for T > 273.16 K, indicating that the direction of spontaneous change is from ice to water, and ΔG is positive for T < 273.16 K, where the reverse reaction of freezing takes place.

ENERGY CONSERVATION

The amount of ATP in a cell is limited, and it must be replaced continually to maintain repair and growth. This is achieved by using the energy liberated during the oxidative stages of catabolism to synthesize ATP from ADP and phosphate. The synthesis of ATP linked to catabolism occurs by two distinct mechanisms: substrate-level phosphorylation and oxidative, or respiratory-chain, phosphorylation. Oxidative phosphorylation is the major method of energy conservation under aerobic conditions in all nonphotosynthetic cells.

SUBSTRATE-LEVEL PHOSPHORYLATION

In substrate-level phosphorylation a phosphoryl group is transferred from an energy-rich donor (e.g., 1,3-diphosphoglycerate) to ADP to yield a molecule of ATP. This type of ATP synthesis does not require molecular oxygen (O_2), although it is frequently, but not always, preceded by an oxidation (i.e., dehydrogenation) reaction. Substrate-level phosphorylation is the major method of energy conservation in oxygen-depleted tissues and during fermentative growth of microorganisms.

OXIDATIVE, OR RESPIRATORY CHAIN, PHOSPHORYLATION

In oxidative phosphorylation the oxidation of catabolic intermediates by molecular oxygen occurs via a highly ordered series of substances that act as hydrogen and electron carriers. They constitute the electron transfer system, or respiratory (or electron transport) chain. In most animals, plants, and fungi, the electron transfer system is fixed in the membranes of mitochondria. In bacteria (which have no mitochondria) this system is incorporated into the plasma membrane. Sufficient free energy is released to allow the synthesis of ATP.

THE NATURE OF THE RESPIRATORY CHAIN

Four types of hydrogen or electron carriers are known to participate in the respiratory chain, in which they serve to transfer two reducing equivalents (2H) from reduced substrate (AH_2) to molecular oxygen (see reaction [16]). The products are the oxidized substrate (A) and water (H_2O).

Step 16

$$AH2 + \tfrac{1}{2}\,O_2 \longrightarrow A + H_2O$$

The carriers are NAD^+ and, less frequently, $NADP^+$; the flavoproteins FAD and FMN (flavin mononucleotide); ubiquinone (or coenzyme Q); and several types of cytochromes. Each carrier has an oxidized and reduced form (e.g., FAD and $FADH_2$, respectively), the two forms constituting an oxidation-reduction, or redox, couple. Within the respiratory chain each redox couple undergoes cyclic oxidation-reduction—i.e., the oxidized component of the couple accepts reducing equivalents from either a substrate or a reduced carrier preceding it in the series and in turn donates these reducing equivalents to the next oxidized carrier in the sequence. Reducing equivalents are thus transferred from substrates to molecular oxygen by a number of sequential redox reactions.

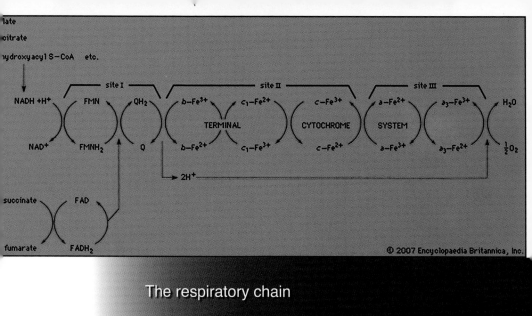

The respiratory chain

Most oxidizable catabolic intermediates initially undergo a dehydrogenation reaction, during which a dehydrogenase enzyme transfers the equivalent of a hydride ion ($H^+ + 2e^-$, with e^- representing an electron) to its coenzyme, either NAD^+ or $NADP^+$. The reduced NAD^+ (or $NADP^+$) thus produced (usually written as $NADH + H^+$ or $NADPH + H^+$) diffuses to the membrane-bound respiratory chain to be oxidized by an enzyme known as NADH dehydrogenase. The enzyme has as its coenzyme FMN. There is no corresponding NADPH dehydrogenase in mammalian mitochondria. Instead, the reducing equivalents of $NADPH + H^+$ are transferred to NAD^+ in a reaction catalyzed by a transhydrogenase enzyme, with the products being reduced $NADH + H^+$ and $NADP^+$. A few substrates (e.g., acyl coenzyme A and succinate) bypass this reaction and instead undergo immediate dehydrogenation by specific membrane-bound

165

dehydrogenase enzymes. During the reaction, the coenzyme FAD accepts two hydrogen atoms and two electrons ($2H + 2e^-$). The reduced flavoproteins (i.e., $FMNH_2$ and $FADH_2$) donate their two hydrogen atoms to the lipid carrier ubiquinone, which is thus reduced.

The fourth type of carrier, the cytochromes, consists of hemoproteins—i.e., proteins with a nonprotein component, or prosthetic group, called heme (or a derivative of heme), which is an iron-containing pigment molecule. The iron atom in the prosthetic group is able to carry one electron and oscillates between the oxidized, or ferric (Fe^{3+}), and the reduced, or ferrous (Fe^{2+}), forms. The five cytochromes present in the mammalian respiratory chain, designated cytochromes b, c_1, c, a, and a_3, act in sequence between ubiquinone and molecular oxygen. The terminal cytochrome of this sequence (a_3, also known as cytochrome oxidase) is able to donate electrons to oxygen rather than to another electron carrier. Cytochrome a_3 is also the site of action of two substances that inhibit the respiratory chain, potassium cyanide and carbon monoxide. Special Fe-S complexes play a role in the activity of NADH dehydrogenase and succinate dehydrogenase.

In each redox couple the reduced form has a tendency to lose reducing equivalents (i.e., to act as an electron or hydrogen donor); similarly, the oxidized form has a tendency to gain reducing equivalents (i.e., to act as an electron or hydrogen acceptor). The oxidation-reduction characteristics of each couple can be determined experimentally under well-defined, standard conditions. The value thus obtained is the standard oxidation-reduction (redox) potential ($E_ó$). Values for respiratory chain carriers range from $E_ó$ = -320 millivolts (1 millivolt = 0.001 volt) for NAD^+/reduced NAD^+ to $E_ó$ = +820 millivolts for $\frac{1}{2}O_2/H_2O$. The values for intermediate carriers lie between. Reduced NAD^+ is the most electronegative carrier, oxygen the most electropositive acceptor. During respiration reducing equivalents undergo stepwise transfer from the reduced form of the most electronegative carrier (reduced NAD^+) to the oxidized form of the most electropositive couple (oxygen). Each step is accompanied by a decline in standard free energy ($\Delta G'$) proportional to the difference in the standard redox potentials (ΔE_0) of the two carriers involved.

Overall oxidation of reduced NAD^+ by oxygen (ΔE_0 = +1,140 millivolts) is accompanied by the liberation of free energy ($\Delta G'$ = -52.4 kilocalories per mole). In theory this energy is sufficient to allow the synthesis of six or seven molecules of ATP. In the cell, however, this synthesis of ATP, called oxidative phosphorylation, proceeds with an efficiency of about 46 percent. Thus only three molecules of ATP are produced per atom of oxygen consumed—this being the so-called $P/2e^-$, P/O, or ADP/O ratio. The energy that is not conserved as ATP is lost as heat. The oxidation of succinate by molecular oxygen (ΔE_0 = +790 millivolts), which is accompanied by a smaller liberation of free energy ($\Delta G'$ = -36.5 kilocalories per mole), yields only two molecules of ATP per atom of oxygen consumed (P/O = 2).

ATP Synthesis in Mitochondria

In order to understand the mechanism by which the energy released during respiration is conserved as ATP, it is necessary to appreciate the structural features of mitochondria. These are organelles in animal and plant cells in which oxidative phosphorylation takes place. There are many mitochondria in animal tissues. For example, heart and skeletal muscle contain many mitochondria, since these tissues require large amounts of energy for mechanical work. Mitochondria are also abundant in the pancreas, where there is biosynthesis, and in the kidney, where the process of excretion begins. Mitochondria have an outer membrane, which allows the passage of most small molecules and ions, and a highly folded inner membrane (crista), which does not even allow the passage of small ions and so maintains a closed space within the cell. The electron-transferring molecules of the respiratory chain and the enzymes responsible for ATP synthesis are located in and on this inner membrane, while the space inside (matrix) contains the enzymes of the TCA cycle (reactions [1] to [13]). The enzyme systems primarily responsible for the release and subsequent oxidation of reducing equivalents are thus closely related so that the reduced coenzymes formed during catabolism (NADH + H$^+$ and FADH$_2$) are available as substrates for respiration. The movement of most charged metabolites into the matrix space is mediated by special carrier proteins in the crista that catalyze exchange-diffusion (i.e., a one-for-one exchange). The oxidative phosphorylation systems of bacteria are similar in principle but show a greater diversity in the composition of their respiratory carriers.

The mechanism of ATP synthesis appears to be as follows. During the transfer of hydrogen atoms from FMNH$_2$ or FADH$_2$ to oxygen, protons (H$^+$ ions) are pumped across the crista from the inside of the mitochondrion to the outside. Thus, respiration generates an electrical potential (and in mitochondria a small pH gradient) across the membrane corresponding to 200 to 300 millivolts, and the chemical energy in the substrate is converted into electrical energy. Attached to the crista is a complex enzyme (ATP synthetase) that binds ATP, ADP, and P$_i$. It has nine polypeptide chain subunits of five different kinds in a cluster and a unit of at least three more membrane proteins composing the attachment point of

ADP and P_i. This complex forms a specific proton pore in the membrane. When ADP and P_i are bound to ATP synthetase, the excess of protons (H^+) that has formed outside of the mitochondria (an H^+ gradient) moves back into the mitochondrion through the enzyme complex. The energy released is used to convert ADP and P_i to ATP. In this process, electrical energy is converted to chemical energy, and it is the supply of ADP that limits the rate of this process. The precise mechanism by which the ATP synthetase complex converts the energy stored in the electrical H^+ gradient to the chemical bond energy in ATP is not fully understood. The H^+ gradient may power other endergonic (energy-requiring) processes besides ATP synthesis, such as the movement of bacterial cells and the transport of carbon substrates or ions.

CHAPTER

5

ANABOLISM

The biosynthesis of cell components (anabolism) may be regarded as occurring in two main stages. In the first, intermediate compounds of the central routes of metabolism are diverted from further catabolism and are channeled into pathways that usually lead to the formation of the relatively small molecules that serve as the building blocks, or precursors, of macromolecules.

In the second stage of biosynthesis, the building blocks are combined to yield the macromolecules—proteins, nucleic acids, lipids, and polysaccharides—that make up the bulk of tissues and cellular components. In organisms with the appropriate genetic capability, for example, all of the amino acids can be synthesized from ammonia and intermediates of the main routes of carbohydrate fragmentation and oxidation. Such intermediates act also as precursors for the purines, the pyrimidines, and the pentose sugars that constitute DNA and for a number of types of RNA. The assembly of proteins necessitates the precise combination of specific amino acids in a highly ordered and controlled manner. This in turn involves the copying, or transcription, into RNA of specific parts of DNA.

The first stage of biosynthesis thus requires the specificity normally required for the efficient functioning of sequences of enzyme-catalyzed reactions. The second stage also involves—directly for protein and nucleic acid synthesis, less directly for the synthesis of other macromolecules—the maintenance and expression of the biological information that specifies the identity of the cell, the tissue, and the organism.

THE STAGES OF BIOSYNTHESIS

The two stages of biosynthesis—the formation of building blocks and their specific assembly into macromolecules—are energy-consuming pro-cesses and thus require ATP. Although the ATP is derived from catabolism, catabolism does not "drive" biosynthesis. The occurrence of chemical reactions in the living cell is accompanied by a net decrease in free energy. Although biological growth and development result in the creation of ordered systems from less ordered ones and of complex systems from simpler ones, these events must occur at the expense of energy-yielding reactions. The overall coupled reactions are, on balance, still accompanied by a decrease in free energy and are thus essentially irreversible in the direction of bio-synthesis. The total energy released from ATP, for example, is usually much greater than is needed for a particular biosynthetic step. Thus, many of the reactions involved in biosynthesis release inorganic pyrophosphate (PP_i) rather than phos-phate (P_i) from ATP, and hence yield AMP rather than ADP. Since inorganic pyrophosphate readily undergoes virtually irreversible hydrolysis to two equivalents of inorganic phosphate, the creation of a new bond in the product of synthesis may be accompanied by the breaking of two high-energy bonds of ATP—although, in theory, one might have sufficed.

The efficient utilization for anabolic processes of ATP and some intermediate compound formed during a catabolic reaction requires the cell to have simultaneously a milieu favourable for both ATP gen-eration and consumption. Catabolism occurs readily only if sufficient ADP is available, and hence, the con-centration of ATP is low. On the other hand, biosyn-thesis requires a high level of ATP and consequently low levels of ADP and AMP. Suitable conditions for the simultaneous function of both processes are met in two ways. Biosynthetic reactions often take place in compartments within the cell different from those in which catabolism occurs. There is thus a physical separation of energy-requiring and energy-yielding processes. Furthermore, biosynthetic reactions are regulated independently of the mechanisms by which catabolism is controlled. Such independent control is made possible by the fact that catabolic and anabolic pathways are not identical. The pacemaker, or key, enzyme that controls the overall rate of a catabolic route usually does not play any role in the biosynthetic pathway of a compound. Similarly, the pacemaker enzymes of biosynthesis are not involved in catabolism. Rather, catabolic pathways are often regulated by the relative amounts of ATP, ADP, and AMP in the cellular compartment in which the pacemaker enzymes are located. In general, ATP inhibits and ADP (or AMP) stimulates such enzymes. In contrast, many biosynthetic routes are regulated by the concentration of the end products of particular anabolic processes, so that the cell synthesizes only as much of these building blocks as it needs.

THE SUPPLY OF BIOSYNTHETIC PRECURSORS

When higher animals consume a mixed diet, sufficient quantities of compounds for both biosynthesis and energy supply are available. Carbohydrates yield intermediates of glycolysis and of the phosphogluconate pathway, which in turn yield acetyl coenzyme A; lipids yield glycolytic intermediates and acetyl coenzyme A; and many amino acids form intermediates of both the TCA cycle and glycolysis. Any intermediate withdrawn for biosynthesis can thus be readily replenished by the catabolism of further nutrients. This situation does not always hold, however. Microorganisms in particular can derive all of their carbon and energy requirements by utilizing a single carbon source. The sole carbon source may be a substance such as a carbohydrate or a fatty acid, or an intermediate of the TCA cycle (or a substance readily converted to one). In both cases, reactions ancillary to those discussed thus far must occur before the carbon source can be utilized.

ANAPLEROTIC ROUTES

Although the catabolism of carbohydrates can occur via a variety of routes, all give rise to pyruvate. During the catabolism of pyruvate, one carbon atom is lost as carbon dioxide and the remaining two form acetyl coenzyme A, which is involved in the TCA cycle. Because the TCA cycle is initiated by the condensation of acetyl coenzyme A with oxaloacetate, which is regenerated in each turn of the cycle, the removal of any intermediate from the cycle would cause the cycle to stop. Yet, various essential cell components are derived from α-oxoglutarate, succinyl coenzyme A, and oxaloacetate, so that these compounds are, in fact, removed from the cycle. Microbial growth with a carbohydrate as the sole carbon source is thus possible only if a cellular process occurs that effects the net formation of some TCA cycle intermediate from an intermediate of carbohydrate catabolism. Such a process, which replenishes the TCA cycle, has been described as an anaplerotic reaction.

Step 1

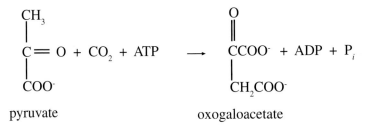

The anaplerotic function may be carried out by either of two enzymes that catalyze the fixation of carbon dioxide onto a three-carbon compound, either pyruvate [1] or phosphoenolpyruvate (PEP, [1a]) to form oxaloacetate, which has four carbon atoms. Both reactions require energy. In [1] it is supplied by the cleavage of ATP to ADP and inorganic phosphate (P_i). In [1a] it is supplied by the release of the high-energy phosphate of PEP as inorganic phosphate.

Pyruvate serves as a carbon dioxide acceptor not only in many bacteria and fungi but also in the livers and kidneys of higher organisms, including humans. PEP serves as the carbon dioxide acceptor in many bacteria, such as those that inhabit the gut.

Step 1a

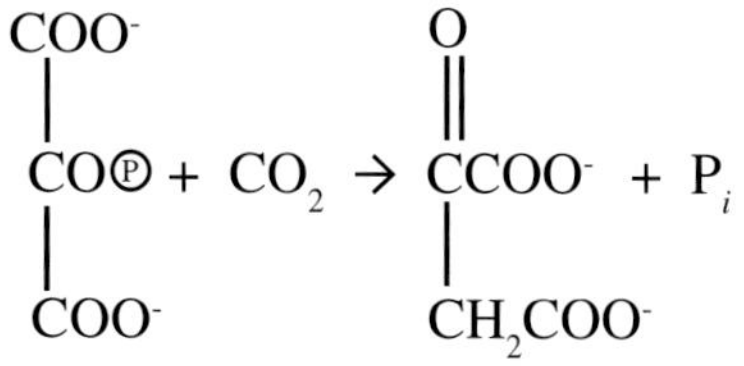

$$\begin{array}{ccc}
COO^- & & O \\
| & & \parallel \\
CO^{\circledP} + CO_2 & \rightarrow & CCOO^- + P_i \\
| & & | \\
COO^- & & CH_2COO^- \\
\end{array}$$

$$\qquad PEP \qquad\qquad\qquad oxaloacetate$$

Unlike higher organisms, many bacteria and fungi can grow on acetate or compounds such as ethanol or a fatty acid that can be catabolized to acetyl coenzyme A. Under these conditions, the net formation of TCA cycle intermediates proceeds in one of two ways. In obligate anaerobic bacteria, pyruvate can be formed from acetyl coenzyme A and carbon dioxide [2]. Reducing equivalents [2H] are necessary for the reaction. The pyruvate so formed can then react via either step [1] or [1a].

Reaction [2] does not occur in facultative anaerobic organisms or in strict aerobes, however.

Step 2

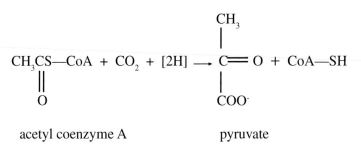

acetyl coenzyme A   pyruvate

Instead, in these organisms two molecules of acetyl coenzyme A give rise to the net synthesis of a four-carbon intermediate of the TCA cycle via a route known as the glyoxylate cycle. In this route, the steps of the TCA cycle that lead to the loss of carbon dioxide are bypassed. Instead of being oxidized to oxalosuccinate, isocitrate is split by isocitrate lyase [3] in a reaction similar to that of carbohydrate fragmentation. The dotted line in [3] indicates the way in which isocitrate is split. The products are succinate and glyoxylate. Glyoxylate, like oxaloacetate, is the anion of an α-oxoacid and thus can condense, in a reaction catalyzed by malate synthase, with acetyl coenzyme A.

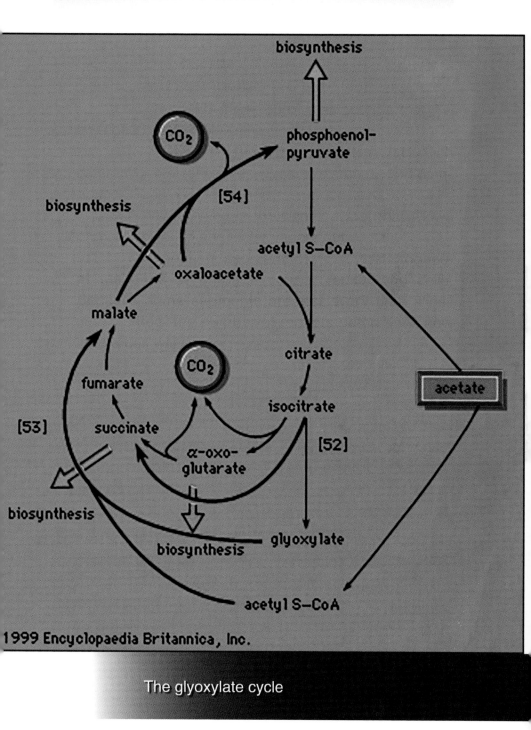

The glyoxylate cycle

Step 3

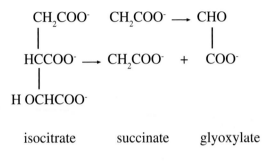

isocitrate succinate glyoxylate

The products of this reaction are coenzyme A and malate [4].

Step 4

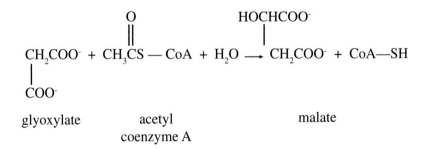

glyoxylate   acetyl   malate
      coenzyme A

In conjunction with the reactions of the TCA cycle that effect the re-formation of isocitrate from malate, steps [3] and [4] lead to the net production of a four-carbon compound (malate) from two two-carbon units (glyoxylate and acetyl coenzyme A). The sequence thus complements the TCA cycle, enabling the cycle to fulfill the dual roles of providing both energy and biosynthetic building blocks when the sole carbon source is a two-carbon compound such as acetate.

GROWTH OF MICROORGANISMS ON TCA CYCLE INTERMEDIATES

Most aerobic microorganisms grow readily on substances such as succinate or malate as their sole source of carbon. Under these circumstances, the formation of the intermediates of carbohydrate metabolism requires an enzymatic step ancillary to the central pathways. In most cases this step is catalyzed by phosphoenolpyruvate (PEP) carboxykinase [5]. Oxaloacetate is decarboxylated (i.e., carbon dioxide is removed) during this energy-requiring reaction. The energy may be supplied by ATP or a similar substance (e.g., GTP) that can readily be derived from it. The products are PEP, carbon dioxide, and ADP.

Step 5

$$\underset{\text{oxaloacetate}}{\overset{\displaystyle O}{\underset{\displaystyle |}{\overset{\displaystyle \|}{C}}COO^- }} + ATP \longrightarrow \underset{\text{PEP}}{\overset{\displaystyle COO^-}{CO\circledP}} + CO2 + ADP$$

O
‖
CCOO⁻ + ATP ⟶ CO℗ + CO2 + ADP
|
CH₂COO⁻   CH₂

oxaloacetate   PEP

Another reaction that can yield an intermediate of carbohydrate catabolism is catalyzed by the so-called malic enzyme. In this reaction, malate is decarboxylated to pyruvate, with concomitant reduction of $NADP^+$ [6]. The primary role of malic enzyme, however, may be to generate reduced $NADP^+$ for biosynthesis rather than to form an intermediate of carbohydrate catabolism.

Step 6

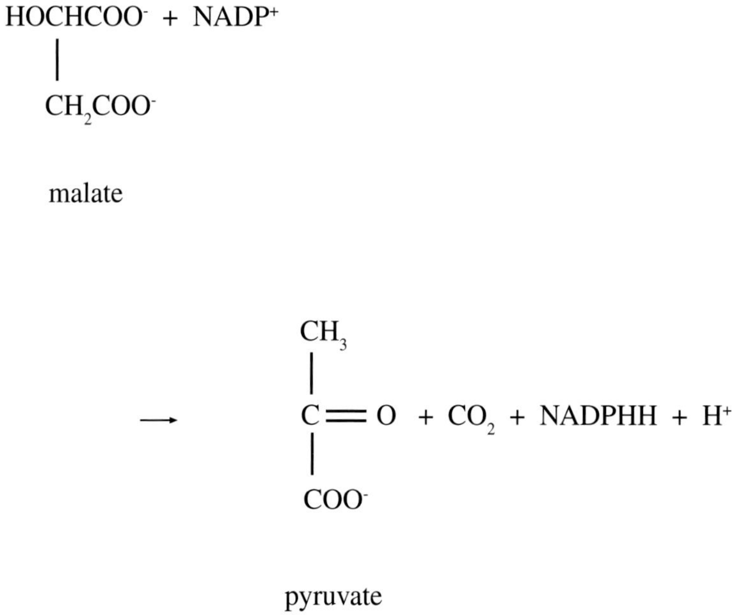

$HOCHCOO^-$ + $NADP^+$

|

CH_2COO^-

malate

$$\longrightarrow \quad \begin{array}{c} CH_3 \\ | \\ C == O \\ | \\ COO^- \end{array} + CO_2 + NADPHH + H^+$$

pyruvate

THE SYNTHESIS OF BUILDING BLOCKS

The basic chemical components of living organisms include sugars (carbohydrates), lipids, amino acids, and mononucleotides. Each of these substances serves as a building block for larger components, and each is synthesized from small, precursor molecules. There are various processes by which these components may be synthesized, among the best characterized of which is gluconeogenesis, which is important in the formation of sugars.

SUGARS

The formation of sugars from noncarbohydrate precursors, gluconeogenesis, is of major importance in all living organisms. In the light, photosynthetic plants and microorganisms incorporate, or fix, carbon dioxide onto a five-carbon sugar and, via a sequence of transfer reactions, re-form the same sugar while also effecting the net synthesis of the glycolytic intermediate, 3-phosphoglycerate. Phosphoglycerate is the precursor of starch, cell-wall carbohydrates, and other plant polysaccharides. A situation similar in principle applies to the growth of microorganisms on precursors of acetyl coenzyme A or on intermediates of the TCA cycle—that is, a large variety of cell components are derived from carbohydrates that, in turn, are synthesized from these noncarbohydrate precursors. Higher organisms also readily convert glucogenic amino acids (i.e., those that do not yield acetyl coenzyme A as a catabolic product) into TCA cycle intermediates, which are then converted into glucose. The amounts of glucose thus transformed depend on the needs of the organism for protein synthesis and on the availability of fuels other than glucose. The synthesis of blood glucose from lactate, which occurs largely in liver, is a particularly active process during recovery from intense muscular activity.

Most of the steps in the pathway for the biosynthesis of glucose from pyruvate are catalyzed by the enzymes of glycolysis, in which the direction of the reactions is reversed. Three virtually irreversible steps in glucose catabolism (the steps for the conversion of phosphoenolpyruvate to pyruvate; the formation of fructose 1,6-diphosphate; and the formation of glucose 6-phosphate and ADP) that cannot be utilized in gluconeogenesis, however, are bypassed by alternative reactions that tend to proceed in the direction of glucose synthesis.

FORMATION OF PEP FROM PYRUVATE

The first alternative reaction is the conversion of pyruvate to PEP. Three mechanisms for overcoming

RESEARCH ON GLUCOSE METABOLISM

The 1947 Nobel Prize for Physiology or Medicine was divided to recognize two discoveries related to glucose metabolism. Argentine physiologist Bernardo Alberto Houssay (1887–1971) was noted for discovering how pituitary hormones regulate the amount of blood sugar (glucose) in animals. American biochemists Carl Cori (1896–1984) and Gerty Cori (1896–1957) were a husband-and-wife team whose discovery of a phosphate-containing form of the simple sugar glucose, and its universal importance to carbohydrate metabolism, led to an understanding of hormonal influence on the interconversion of sugars and starches in the animal organism.

Working with dogs that had been rendered diabetic by excision of the pancreas (1924–37), Houssay found that removal of the adenohypophysis (the anterior, or frontal, lobe of the pituitary body, located beneath the brain) greatly relieved the symptoms of the disease and made the animal unusually sensitive to insulin. He demonstrated that injection of pituitary extracts into normal animals induces diabetes by increasing the amount of sugar in the blood, indicating that the secretions of the gland oppose the action of insulin.

Appointed a professor of physiology in 1910 and the director of the physiological institute at the University of Buenos Aires in 1919, Houssay was one of 150 Argentine educators dismissed from their posts by the 1943 military coup of General Juan Perón.

(continued on the next page)

(continued from the previous page)

Although he was reinstated in 1945, he was asked to submit his resignation a year later. He founded (1944) and directed (from 1946) the privately funded Institute of Biology and Experimental Medicine in Buenos Aires, a leading physiological research centre.

Carl and Gerty Cori met while students at the German University of Prague and were married in 1920, receiving their medical degrees the same year. Immigrating to the United States in 1922, they joined the staff of the Institute for the Study of Malignant Disease, Buffalo, N.Y. (1922–31). As faculty members of the Washington University medical school, St. Louis (from 1931), they discovered (1936) the activated intermediate, glucose 1-phosphate (phosphate bound to a specific carbon atom on the glucose molecule), known as the "Cori ester." They demonstrated that it represents the first step in the conversion into glucose of the animal storage carbohydrate glycogen, large quantities of which are found in the liver, and— because the reaction is reversible—in some cases the last step in the conversion of blood glucose to glycogen.

Six years later they isolated and purified the enzyme (glycogen phosphorylase) responsible for catalyzing the glycogen-Cori ester reaction, and with it they achieved the test-tube synthesis of glycogen in 1943. Proof of the interconversion allowed them to formulate the "Cori cycle," postulating that liver glycogen is converted to blood glucose that is reconverted to glycogen in muscle, where its breakdown to lactic acid provides the energy utilized in muscle contraction. The lactic acid is used to re-form glycogen in the liver. Studying the way in which hormones affect carbohydrate metabolism in animals, the Coris showed that epinephrine induces the formation of a type of phosphorylase enzyme favouring conversion of glycogen to activated glucose and that insulin causes the removal of sugar from the blood by promoting the addition of phosphate to glucose. The Coris trained a large number of graduate students and postdoctoral fellows from all over the world. After his wife's death Carl Cori devoted his efforts to research concerning the physico-chemical action of enzymes involved in the breakdown of glycogen to lactic acid.

the energy barrier associated with the direct reversal of the pyruvate kinase are known. In some bacteria, PEP is formed from pyruvate by the utilization of two of the high-energy bonds of ATP. The products of this reaction include, in addition to PEP, AMP and inorganic phosphate [7]. A variant of this reaction occurs in some bacteria, in which ATP and inorganic phosphate are reactants and AMP and inorganic pyrophosphate are products. Inorganic pyrophosphate is likely to be hydrolyzed to two equivalents of inorganic phosphate, so that the net balance of the reaction is identical with [7].

Step 7

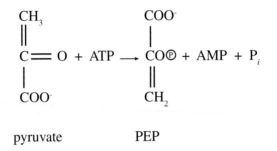

pyruvate   PEP

In other organisms, including many microorganisms, birds, and mammals, the formation of PEP from pyruvate is effected by the sum of reactions [1] and [5], each of which consumes one ATP. The overall balance is shown in [8], in which two molecules of ATP react with pyruvate to form PEP, ADP, and inorganic phosphate. The enzyme adenylate kinase catalyzes the interconversion of the various adenine nucleotides, as shown in [9].

Step 8

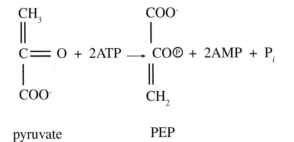

pyruvate   PEP

The combination of steps [8] and [9] yields the same energy balance as does the direct conversion of pyruvate to PEP [7].

Step 9

$$2ADP \rightleftharpoons ATP + AMP$$

HYDROLYSIS OF FRUCTOSE 1, 6-DIPHOSPHATE AND GLUCOSE 6-PHOSPHATE

The second step of glycolysis bypassed in gluconeogenesis is that catalyzed by phosphofructokinase. Instead, the fructose 1,6-diphosphate synthesized from dihydroxyacetonephosphate and glyceraldehyde 3-phosphate in the reaction catalyzed by aldolase is hydrolyzed, with the loss of the phosphate group linked to the first carbon atom.

Step 10

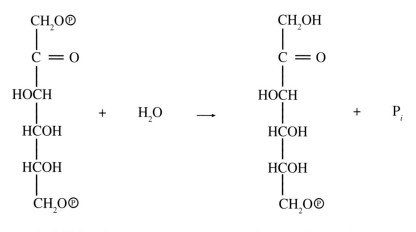

fructose 1, 6-diphosphate   fructose 6-phosphate

The enzyme fructose diphosphatase catalyzes the reaction [10], in which the products are fructose 6-phosphate and inorganic phosphate. The fructose 6-phosphate thus formed is a precursor of mucopolysaccharides (polysaccharides with nitrogen-containing components). In addition, its conversion to glucose 6-phosphate provides the starting material for the formation of storage polysaccharides such as starch and glycogen, of monosaccharides other than glucose, of disaccharides (carbohydrates with two sugar components), and of some structural polysaccharides (e.g., cellulose). The maintenance of the glucose content of vertebrate blood requires glucose 6-phosphate to be converted to glucose. This process occurs in the kidney, in the lining of the intestine, and most importantly in the liver. The reaction does not occur by reversal of the hexokinase or glucokinase reactions that effect the formation of glucose 6-phosphate from glucose and ATP. Rather, glucose 6-phosphate is hydrolyzed in a reaction catalyzed by glucose 6-phosphatase, and the phosphate is released as inorganic phosphate [11].

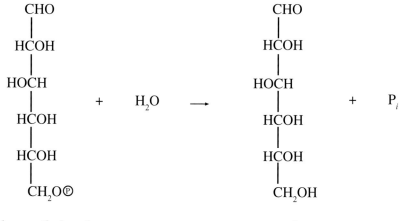

glucose 6-phosphate   glucose

LIPID COMPONENTS

The component building blocks of the lipids found in storage fats, in lipoproteins (combinations of lipid and protein), and in the membranes of cells and organelles are glycerol, the fatty acids, and a number of other compounds (e.g., serine, inositol). Glycerol is readily derived from dihydroxyacetone phosphate, an intermediate of glycolysis. In a reaction catalyzed by glycerol 1-phosphate dehydrogenase [12], dihydroxyacetone phosphate is reduced to glycerol 1-phosphate. Reduced NAD^+ provides the reducing equivalents for the reaction and is oxidized. This compound reacts further.

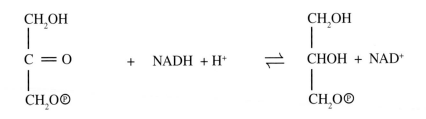

dihydroxyacetone phosphate

glycerol 1-phosphate

Although all the carbon atoms of the fatty acids found in lipids are derived from the acetyl coenzyme A produced by the catabolism of carbohydrates and fatty acids, the molecule first undergoes a carboxylation, forming malonyl coenzyme A, before participating in fatty acid synthesis. The carboxylation reaction is catalyzed by acetyl CoA carboxylase, an enzyme whose prosthetic group is the vitamin biotin. The biotin–enzyme first undergoes a reaction that results in the attachment of carbon dioxide to biotin. ATP is required and forms ADP and inorganic phosphate [13a]. The complex product, called carboxybiotin–enzyme, releases the carboxy moiety to acetyl coenzyme A, forming malonyl coenzyme A and restoring the biotin–enzyme [13b].

Step 13a

$$\text{biotin — enzyme} + \text{ATP} + CO_2 \quad \rightleftharpoons$$

$$^-OOC - \text{biotin-enzyme} + \text{ADP} + P_i$$

carboxybiotin-enzyme

Step 13b

$$^-OOC - \text{biotin — enzyme} + CH_3CS - CoA \quad \rightleftharpoons$$
$$\underset{O}{\overset{\|}{}}$$

carboxybiotin-   acetyl coenzyme A
enzyme

$$\begin{array}{c} COO^- \\ | \\ CH_2CS - CoA \\ \| \\ O \end{array} + \text{biotin-enzyme}$$

malonyl coenzyme

The overall reaction [13] catalyzed by acetyl coenzyme A carboxylase thus involves the expenditure of one molecule of ATP for the formation of each molecule of malonyl coenzyme A from acetyl coenzyme A and carbon dioxide.

193

$$CH_2CS \!-\! CoA + CO_2 + ATP \quad \rightleftharpoons$$
$$\underset{O}{\overset{\|}{}}$$

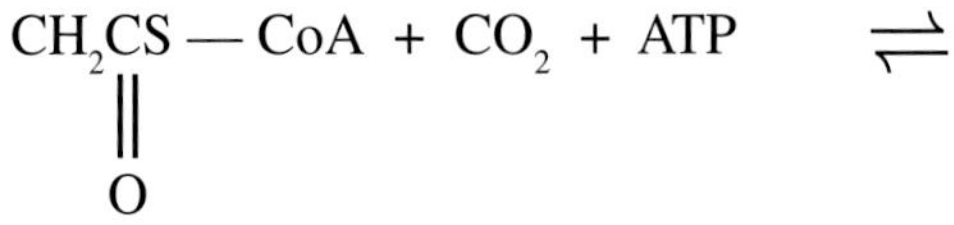

acetyl coenzyme A

$$\overset{COO-}{\underset{\|}{\underset{O}{|}}}CH_2CS \!-\! CoA + ADP + P_i$$

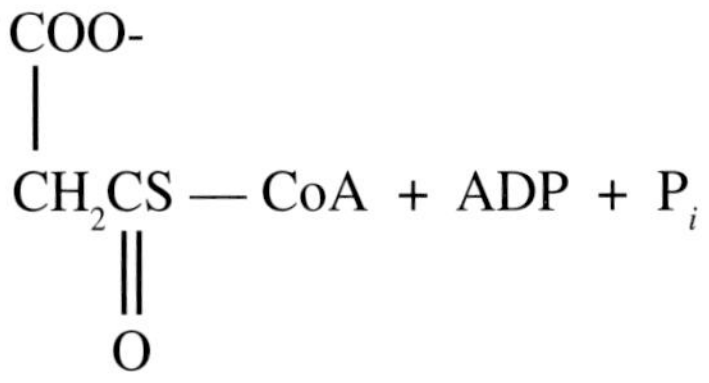

malonyl coenzyme A

Malonyl coenzyme A and a molecule of acetyl coenzyme A react (in bacteria) with the sulfhydryl group of a relatively small molecule known as acyl-carrier protein (ACP–SH). In higher organisms ACP–SH is part of a multienzyme complex called fatty acid synthetase. ACP–SH is involved in all of the reactions leading to the synthesis of a fatty acid such as palmitic acid from acetyl coenzyme A and malonyl coenzyme A. The products of [14a] and [14b] are acetyl-S-ACP, malonyl-S-ACP, and coenzyme A. The enzymes catalyzing [14a] and [14b] are known as acetyl transacylase and malonyl transacylase, respectively.

Acetyl-ACP and malonyl-ACP react in a reaction catalyzed by β-ketoacyl-ACP synthetase so that the acetyl moiety (CH_3CO-) is transferred to the malonyl moiety (-$OOCH_2CO$-). Simultaneously, the carbon dioxide fixed in step [13] is lost, leaving as a product a four-carbon moiety attached to ACP and called acetoacetyl-S-ACP [15].

Step 14

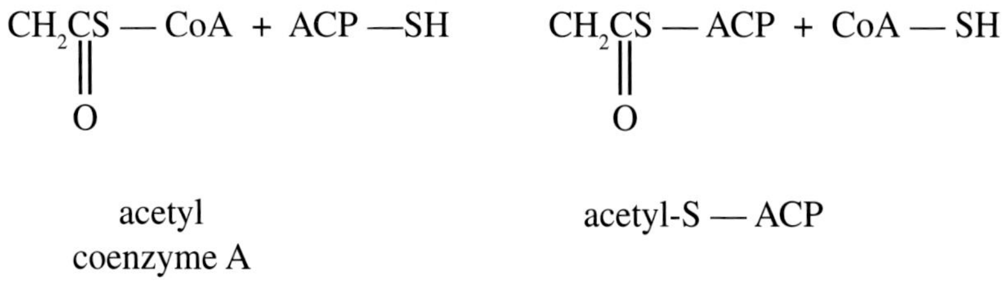

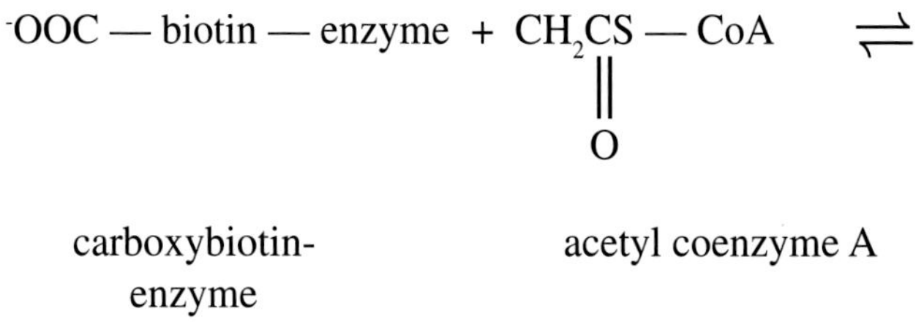

$$CH_2CS \!-\! CoA \;+\; ACP \!-\! SH \qquad CH_2CS \!-\! ACP \;+\; CoA \!-\! SH$$

$$\underset{O}{\|} \qquad\qquad\qquad\qquad\qquad \underset{O}{\|}$$

acetyl   acetyl-S — ACP

coenzyme A

$$^-OOC \!-\! biotin \!-\! enzyme \;+\; CH_2CS \!-\! CoA \qquad \rightleftharpoons$$

$$\underset{O}{\|}$$

carboxybiotin-   acetyl coenzyme A

enzyme

Step 14b

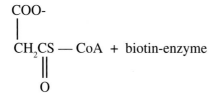

$$COO^-$$
$$|$$
$$CH_2CS \!-\! CoA \;+\; biotin\text{-}enzyme$$
$$\underset{O}{\|}$$

malonyl coenzyme A   malonyl-S — ACP

It should be noted that the carbon atoms of acetyl-SACP occur at the end of acetoacetyl-S-ACP (see carbon atoms numbered 4 and 3 in [15]) and that carbon dioxide plays an essentially catalytic role. The decarboxylation of the malonyl-S-ACP [15] provides a strong thermodynamic pull toward fatty acid synthesis.

Step 15

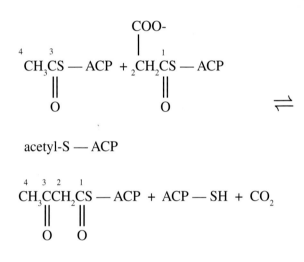

$$\underset{4}{CH_3}\underset{3}{CS} - ACP + \underset{2}{CH_2}\underset{1}{CS} - ACP \quad \overset{COO-}{\underset{1}{\big|}} \rightleftharpoons$$

acetyl-S — ACP

$$\underset{4}{CH_3}\underset{3}{C}\underset{2}{CH_2}\underset{1}{CS} - ACP + ACP - SH + CO_2$$

acetoacetyl-S — ACP

The analogy between fatty acid synthesis and the cleavage of fatty acid catabolism is apparent in the other reactions of fatty acid synthesis. The acetoacetyl-S-ACP, for example, undergoes reduction to β-hydroxybutyryl-SACP [16]. The reaction is catalyzed by β-ketoacyl-ACP reductase. Reduced $NADP^+$ is the electron donor, however, and not reduced NAD^+. $NADP^+$

is thus a product in [16]. In [17] β-hydroxybutyryl-S-ACP is dehydrated (i.e., one molecule of water is removed), in a reaction catalyzed by enoyl-ACP-hydrase, and then undergoes a second reduction [18], in which reduced NADP⁺ again acts as the electron donor.

Step 16

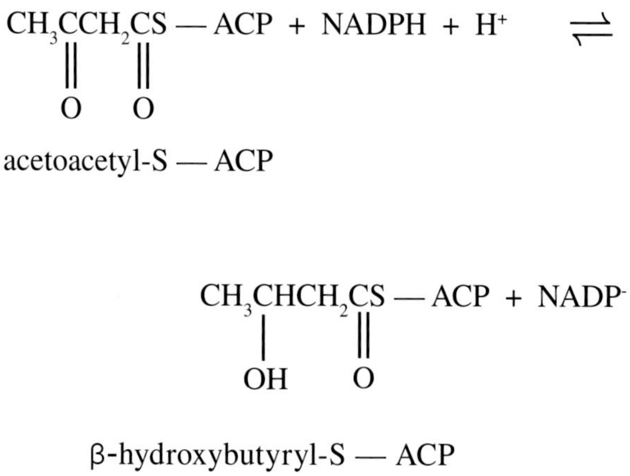

$$CH_3CCH_2CS - ACP + NADPH + H^+ \rightleftharpoons$$
$$\quad\quad\; \| \quad\; \|$$
$$\quad\quad\; O \quad\; O$$

acetoacetyl-S — ACP

$$CH_3CHCH_2CS - ACP + NADP^-$$
$$\quad\quad\; | \quad\quad\; \|$$
$$\quad\quad\; OH \quad\; O$$

β-hydroxybutyryl-S — ACP

The products of [17] are crotonyl-S-ACP and water. The products of [18], which is catalyzed by crotonyl-ACP reductase, are butyryl-S-ACP and NADP⁺.

Step 17

$$CH_3CHCH_2CS - ACP \qquad\qquad CH_3CH = CHCS - ACP + H_2O$$
$$\quad | \quad\quad \| \qquad\qquad\qquad\qquad\qquad \|$$
$$\quad OH \quad O \qquad\qquad\qquad\qquad\qquad O$$

hydroxybutyryl-S — ACP   crotonyl-S — ACP

The formation of butyryl-S-ACP [18] completes the first of several cycles, in each of which one molecule of malonyl coenzyme A enters via reactions [13] and [14b]. In the cycle following the one ending with [18], the butyryl moiety is transferred to malonyl-S-ACP, a molecule of carbon dioxide is again lost, and a six-carbon compound results. In subsequent cycles, each of which adds two carbon atoms to the molecule via reaction [15], successively longer β-oxoacyl-S-ACP derivatives are produced.

Step 18

$$CH_3CH = CHCS - ACP + NADPH + H^+ \rightleftharpoons$$
$$\underset{O}{\overset{\parallel}{}}$$

crotonyl-S — ACP

$$CH_3CH_2CH_2CS - ACP + NADP^+$$
$$\underset{O}{\overset{\parallel}{}}$$

butyryl-S — ACP

Ultimately, a molecule with 16 carbon atoms, palmityl S-ACP, is formed. In most organisms a deacylase catalyzes the release of free palmitic acid. In a few, synthesis continues, and an acid with 18 carbon atoms is formed. The fatty acids can then react with coenzyme A to form fatty acyl coenzyme A, which can condense with the glycerol 1-phosphate formed in step [12]. The product is a phosphatidic acid. The overall formation of each molecule of palmitic acid from acetyl coenzyme A—via step [13] and repeated cycles of steps [14] through [18]—requires the investment of seven molecules of ATP and 14 of reduced NADP+ (see [19]). The process is thus an energy requiring one (endergonic) and represents a major way by which the reducing power generated in NADP-linked dehydrogenation reactions of carbohydrate catabolism is utilized.

Step 19

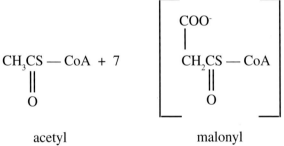

$$CH_3CS-CoA + 7 \quad \begin{bmatrix} COO^- \\ | \\ CH_2CS-CoA \\ || \\ O \end{bmatrix}$$

acetyl coenzyme A   malonyl coenzyme A

$$+ \; 14NADPH + 14H^+ \longrightarrow CH_3(CH_2)_{14}COO^-$$

palmitate

$$+ \; 7CO_2 + 8CoA-SH + 14NADPH^+ + 6H_2O$$

The major lipids that serve as components of membranes, called phospholipids, as well as lipoproteins, contain, in addition to two molecules of fatty acid,

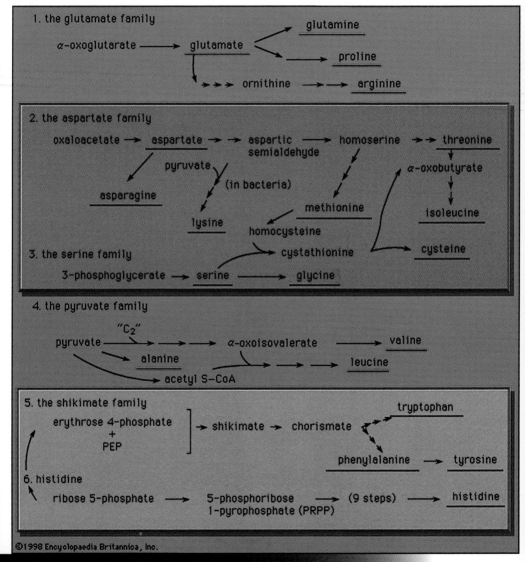

Family relationships in amino-acid biosyntheses. Components of proteins are underlined. Not all of the intermediates formed are named.

one molecule of a variety of different compounds. The precursors of these compounds include serine, inositol, and glycerol 1-phosphate. They are derived from intermediates of the central metabolic pathways.

AMINO ACIDS

Organisms differ considerably in their ability to synthesize amino acids from the intermediates of central metabolic pathways. Most vertebrates can form only the chemically most simple amino acids. The others must be supplied in the diet. Humans, for example, synthesize about 10 of the 20 commonly encountered amino acids. These are known as the nonessential amino acids. The essential amino acids must be supplied in food.

Higher plants are more versatile than animals. They can make all of the amino acids required for protein synthesis, with either ammonia (NH_3) or nitrate (NO_3) as the nitrogen source. Some bacteria, and leguminous plants (e.g., peas) that harbour such bacteria in their root nodules, are able to utilize nitrogen from the air to form ammonia and use the latter for amino-acid synthesis.

Bacteria differ widely in their ability to synthesize amino acids. Some species, such as *Escherichia coli*, which can grow in media supplied with only a single carbon source and ammonium salts, can make all of their amino acids from these starting materials. Other bacteria may require as many as 16 different amino acids.

Each of the 20 common amino acids is synthesized by a different pathway, the complexity of which reflects the chemical complexity of the amino acid formed. As with other compounds, the pathway for the synthesis of an amino acid is for the most part different from that by which it is catabolized.

There are two major features of amino-acid biosynthesis common to the generation of all amino acids. First, ammonia is incorporated into the intermediates of metabolic pathways mainly via glutamate dehydrogenase. Similarly, the transaminase enzymes enable the amino group (NH_2-) to be transferred to other amino acids. Second, a group of several amino acids may be synthesized from one amino acid, which acts as a "parent" of an amino-acid "family." The families are also interrelated in several instances. Alpha-oxoglutarate and oxaloacetate are intermediates of the TCA cycle. Likewise, pyruvate, 3-phosphoglycerate and PEP are intermediates of glycolysis, and ribose 5-phosphate and erythrose 4-phosphate are formed in the phosphogluconate pathway.

NUCLEOTIDES

Most organisms can synthesize the purine and pyrimidine nucleotides that serve as the building blocks of RNA (containing nucleotides in which the pentose sugar is ribose, called ribonucleotides) and DNA (containing nucleotides in which the pentose sugar is deoxyribose, called deoxyribonucleotides) as well as the agents of energy exchange. The purine ribonucleotides (AMP and GMP) are derived from ribose 5-phosphate. The overall sequence that leads to the parent purine ribonucleotide, which is inosinic acid, involves 10 enzymatic steps. Inosinic acid can be converted to AMP and GMP. These in turn yield the triphosphates (i.e., ATP and GTP) via reactions catalyzed by adenylate kinase [20] and nucleoside diphosphate kinase.

Step 20

$$GMP \ + \ ATP \ \rightleftharpoons \ GDP \ + \ ADP$$

The biosynthetic pathway for the pyrimidine nucleotides is somewhat simpler than that for the purine nucleotides. Aspartate (derived from the TCA cycle intermediate, oxaloacetate) and carbamoyl phosphate (derived from carbon dioxide, ATP, and ammonia) condense to form N-carbamoylaspartate [21], which loses water [22] in a reaction catalyzed by dihydroorotase. The product, dihydroorotate, is then oxidized to orotate in a reaction catalyzed by dihydroorotic acid dehydrogenase, in which NAD^+ is reduced [23].

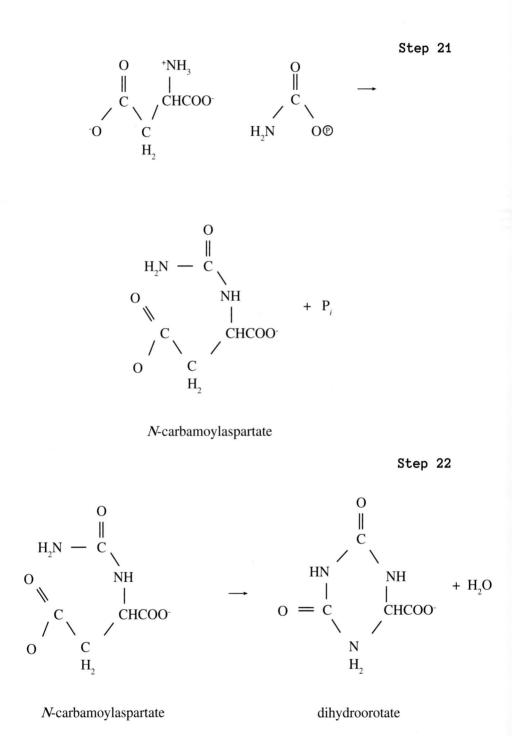

Step 21

N-carbamoylaspartate

+ P$_i$

Step 22

N-carbamoylaspartate

dihydroorotate

+ H$_2$O

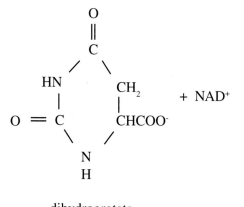

dihydroorotate

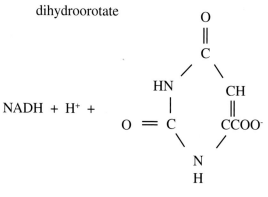

orotate

The orotate accepts a pentose phosphate moiety [24] from 5-phosphoribose 1-pyrophosphate (PRPP). PRPP, which is formed from ribose 5-phosphate and ATP, also initiates the pathways for biosynthesis of purine nucleotides and of histidine. The product loses carbon dioxide to yield the parent pyrimidine nucleotide, uridylic acid (UMP; see [24]).

Analogous to the phosphorylation of purine nucleotides is the phosphorylation of UMP to UDP and thence to UTP by interaction with two molecules of ATP. Uridine triphosphate (UTP) can be converted to the other pyrimidine building block of RNA, cytidine triphosphate (CTP). In bacteria, the nitrogen for this reaction [25] is derived from ammonia. In higher animals, glutamine is the nitrogen donor.

Step 24

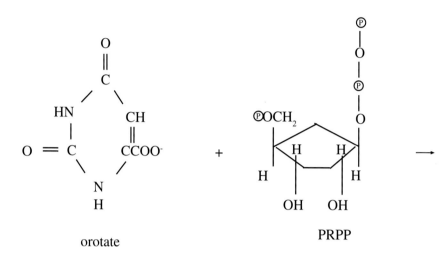

orotate   +   PRPP   →

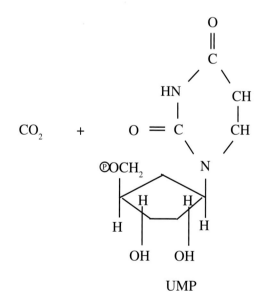

CO_2 +

UMP

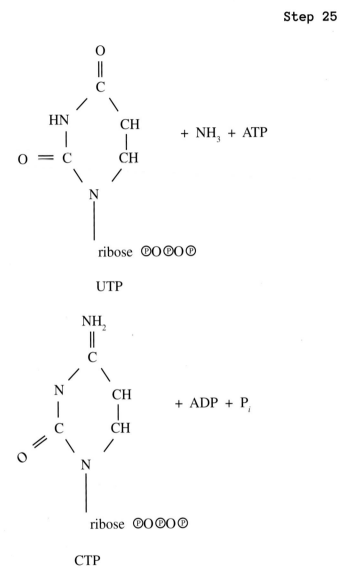

+ NH$_3$ + ATP

UTP

+ ADP + P$_i$

CTP

The building blocks for the synthesis of DNA differ from those for the synthesis of RNA in two

respects. In DNA the purine and pyrimidine nucleotides contain the pentose sugar 2-deoxyribose
instead of ribose. In addition, the pyrimidine base
uracil, found in RNA, is replaced in DNA by thymine. The deoxyribonucleoside diphosphate can be
derived directly from the corresponding ribonucle-
oside diphosphate by a process involving the two
sulfhydryl groups of the protein, thioredoxin, and a
flavoprotein, thioredoxin reductase, that can in turn
be reduced by reduced $NADP^+$. Thus, for the reduction of XDP, in which X represents a purine base
or cytosine, the reaction may be written as shown
in [26a] and [26b]. In [26a] oxidized thioredoxin-S_2
is reduced to thioredoxin-(SH)2 by NADPH, which
is oxidized in the process. Thioredoxin-$(SH)_2$ then
reduces XDP to deoxyXDP in a reaction [26b] in
which thioredoxin is re-formed.

Step 26a

$$\text{thioredoxin-}S_2 + NADPH + H^+ \longrightarrow$$

$$\text{thioredoxin-}(SH)_2 + NADPH^+$$

Step 26b

$$\text{thioredoxin-}(SH)_2 + XDP \longrightarrow$$

$$\text{thioredoxin-}S_2 + \text{deoxyXDP}$$

Deoxythymidylic acid (dTMP) is derived from
deoxyuridylic acid (dUMP).

Step 27

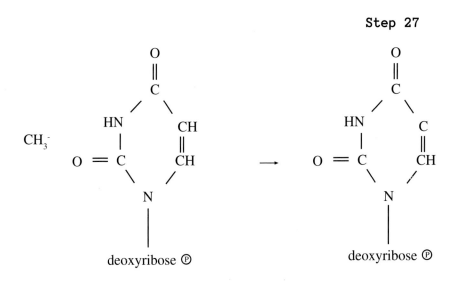

dUMP   dTMP

Deoxyuridine diphosphate (dUDP) is first con-verted to dUMP, by reaction [20] proceeding from right to left. Deoxyuridylic acid then accepts a methyl group (CH_3-) in a reaction catalyzed by an enzyme (thymidylate synthetase) with the vitamin folic acid as a coenzyme. The product of this reaction is dTMP [27].

THE SYNTHESIS OF MACROMOLECULES

The formation of polysaccharides and of phospho-lipids from their component building blocks not only requires the investment of the energy of nucleoside triphosphates but uses these molecules in a novel manner. The biosynthetic reactions described thus far have mainly been accompanied by the formation of energy-rich intermediates with the formation of either

AMP or ADP. However, nucleotides serve as interme-diate carriers in the formation of glycogen, starch, and a variety of lipids.

CARBOHYDRATES AND LIPIDS

This unique process necessitates reactions by which ATP or another nucleoside triphosphate com-bines with a phosphorylated reactant to form a nucleoside-diphosphate product. Although the change in standard free energy is small in this reaction, the sub-sequent hydrolysis of the inorganic pyrophosphate also released effectively makes the reaction irreversible in the direction of synthesis. (The nucleoside triphosphate is represented as NTP in [28], and the phosphorylated reactant as R bound to the encircled P.) Reactions of this type are catalyzed by pyrophosphorylases.

Step 28

$$\text{NTP R} - \text{\textcircled{P}} \rightleftharpoons \text{NDP} - \text{R} + \text{PP}_i$$

FORMATION OF STORAGE POLYSACCHARIDES

In the formation of storage polysaccharides—i.e., glycogen in animals, starch in plants—reaction [28] is preceded by the conversion of glucose 6-phosphate to glucose 1-phosphate, in a reaction catalyzed by phosphoglucomutase [29]. UTP is the specific NTP for glycogen synthesis in animals [28a]. The prod-ucts are UDP-glucose and pyrophosphate.

211

Step 29

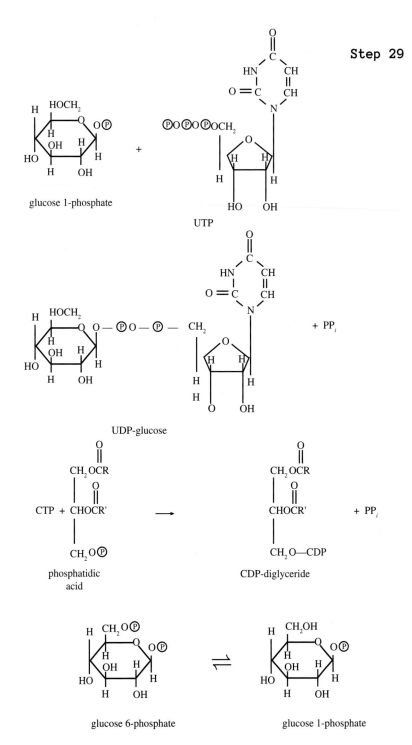

glucose 1-phosphate

UTP

UDP-glucose

+ PP$_i$

CTP + phosphatidic acid → CDP-diglyceride + PP$_i$

glucose 6-phosphate ⇌ glucose 1-phosphate

In bacteria, fungi, and plants, ATP, CTP, or GTP serves instead of UTP. In all cases the nucleoside diphosphate glucose (NDP-glucose) thus synthesized can donate glucose to the terminal glucose of a polysaccharide chain, thereby increasing the number (n) of glucose molecules by one to $n + 1$ [30]. UDP is released in this process, which is catalyzed by glycogen synthetase. Starch synthesis in plants occurs by an analogous pathway catalyzed by amylose synthetase. ADP-glucose rather than UDP-glucose is the preferred glucose donor [30a]. Similarly, cellulose, the major structural polysaccharide in plant cell walls, is synthesized in some plants by reaction [30a]. Other plants undergo analogous reactions in which GDP-glucose or CDP-glucose acts as the glucose donor.

Step 30

$$\text{UDP-glucose} + (\text{glucose})_2 \longrightarrow \text{UDP} + (\text{glucose})_{2+1}$$

Step 30a

$$\text{ADP-glucose} + (\text{glucose})_2 \longrightarrow \text{ADP} + (\text{glucose})_{2+1}$$

Nucleoside diphosphate sugars also participate in the synthesis of disaccharides. For example, common table sugar, sucrose (consisting of glucose and fructose), is formed in sugarcane by the reaction sequence shown in [31] and [32].

Step 31

$$\text{UDP-glucose} + \text{fructose 6-phosphate}$$
$$\longrightarrow \text{UDP} + \text{sucrose 6'-phosphate}$$

Step 32

$$\text{sucrose 6'-phosphate} + H_2O \longrightarrow \text{sucrose} + P_i$$

UDP-glucose and fructose 6-phosphate first form a phosphorylated derivative of sucrose, sucrose 6′-phosphate, which is hydrolyzed to sucrose and inorganic phosphate. Lactose, which consists of galactose and glucose, is the principal sugar of milk. It is synthesized in the mammary gland as shown in [33]. UDP-galactose and glucose react to form lactose. UDP is also a product.

Step 33

$$\text{UDP-glucose} + \text{glucose} \longrightarrow \text{UDP} + \text{lactose}$$

FORMATION OF LIPIDS

The neutral fats, or triglycerides, that constitute storage lipids, and the phospholipid components of lipoproteins and membranes, are synthesized from their building blocks by a route that branches after the first biosynthetic reaction. Initially, one molecule of glycerol 1-phosphate, the intermediate derived from carbohydrate catabolism, and two molecules of the appropriate fatty acyl coenzyme A combine, yielding phosphatidic acid [34].

214

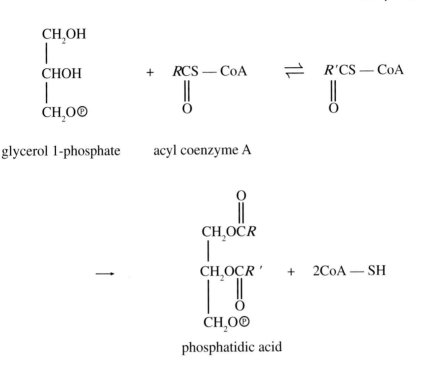

glycerol 1-phosphate   acyl coenzyme A

phosphatidic acid

This reaction occurs preferentially with acyl coenzyme A derivatives of fatty acids containing 16 or 18 carbon atoms. In reaction [34], R and R' represent the hydrocarbon moieties ($Ch_3(CH_2)$ n -) of two fatty acid molecules. A triglyceride molecule (neutral fat) is formed from phosphatidic acid in a reaction catalyzed by a phosphatase that results in loss of the phosphate group [35].

The diglyceride thus formed can then accept a third molecule of fatty acyl coenzyme A [35a].

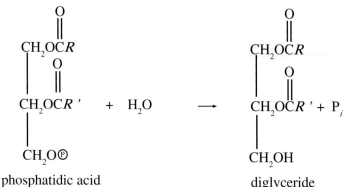

phosphatidic acid   diglyceride

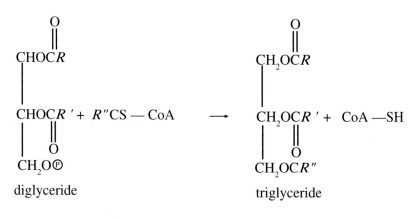

diglyceride   triglyceride

In the biosynthesis of phospholipids, however, phosphatidic acid is not hydrolyzed. Rather, it acts as the R–phosphoryl group (represented by the encircled P) in reaction [28], the NTP here being cytidine triphosphate (CTP). A CDP-diglyceride is produced, and inorganic pyrophosphate is released [28b]. CDP-diglyceride is the common precursor of a variety of phospholipids. In subsequent reactions, each catalyzed by a specific enzyme, CMP is displaced from CDP-diglyceride by one of three compounds—serine, inositol, or glycerol 1-phosphate—to form CMP and, respectively, phosphatidylserine [36a], phosphatidylinositol [36b], or, in [36c], 3-phosphatidylglycerol 1'-phosphate (PGP). These reactions differ from those of polysaccharide biosynthesis ([30], [33]) in that phosphate is retained in the phospholipid, and the nucleotide product (CMP) is therefore a nucleoside monophosphate rather than the diphosphate. These compounds can react further: phosphatidylserine to give, sequentially, phosphatidylethanolamine and phosphatidylcholine; phosphatidylinositol to yield mono and diphosphate derivatives that are components of brain tissue and of mitochondrial membranes; and PGP to yield the phosphatidylglycerol abundant in many bacterial membranes and the diphosphatidylglycerol that is also a major component of mitochondrial and bacterial membranes.

Step 36a

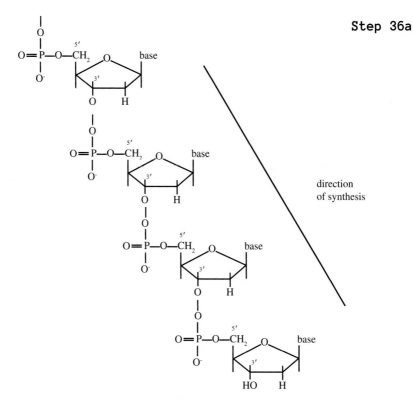

direction
of synthesis

(free 3′-hydroxyl end)

DNA strand

Step 36b

CDP-diglyceride + inositol $\longrightarrow$ phosphatidylinositol + CMP

Step 36c

CDP-diglyceride + glycerol 1-phosphate $\longrightarrow$ PGP + CMP

NUCLEIC ACIDS AND PROTEINS

As with the synthesis of polysaccharides and lipids, the formation of the nucleic acids and proteins from their building blocks requires the input of energy. Nucleic acids are formed from nucleoside triphosphates, with concomitant elimination of inorganic pyrophosphate, which is subsequently hydrolyzed. Amino acids also are activated, forming, at the expense of ATP, aminoacyl-complexes. This activation process is also accompanied by loss of inorganic pyrophosphate. But, although these biochemical processes are basically similar to those involved in the biosynthesis of other macromolecules, their occurrence is specifically subservient to the genetic information in DNA. DNA contains within its structure the blueprint both for its own exact duplication and for the synthesis of a number of types of RNA, among which is a class termed messenger RNA (mRNA). A complementary relationship exists between the sequence of purines (i.e., adenine and guanosine) and pyrimidines (cytosine and thymine) in the DNA comprising a gene and the sequence in mRNA into which this genetic information is transcribed. This information is then translated into the sequence of amino acids in a protein, a process that involves the functioning of a variety of other classes of ribonucleic acids.

REGULATION OF METABOLISM

The flux of nutrients along each metabolic pathway is governed chiefly by two factors: (1) the availability of substrates on which pacemaker, or key, enzymes of the pathway can act and (2) the intracellular levels of specific metabolites that affect the reaction rates of pacemaker enzymes. Key enzymes are usually complex proteins that, in addition to the site at which the catalytic process occurs (i.e., the active site), contain sites to which the regulatory metabolites bind. Interactions with the appropriate molecules at these regulatory sites cause changes in the shape of the enzyme molecule. Such changes may either facilitate or hinder the changes that occur at the active site. The rate of the enzymatic reaction is thus speeded up or slowed down by the presence of a regulatory metabolite.

FINE CONTROL

In many cases, the specific small molecules that bind to the regulatory sites have no obvious structural similarity to the substrates of the enzymes. These small molecules are therefore called allosteric effectors, and the regulatory sites are known as allosteric sites. Allosteric effectors may be formed by enzyme-catalyzed reactions in the same pathway in which the enzyme regulated by the effectors functions. In this case a rise in the level of the allosteric effector would affect the flux of nutrients along that pathway in a manner analogous to the feedback phenomena of homeostatic processes. Such effectors may also be formed by enzymatic reactions in apparently unrelated pathways. In this instance the rate at which one metabolic pathway operates would be profoundly affected by the rate of nutrient flux along another. It is this situation that, to a large extent, governs the sensitive and immediately responsive coordination of the many metabolic routes in the cell.

End-Product Inhibition

A biosynthetic pathway is usually controlled by an allosteric effector produced as the end product of that pathway, and the pacemaker enzyme on which the effector acts usually catalyzes the first step that uniquely leads to the end product. This phenomenon, called end-product inhibition, is illustrated by the multienzyme, branched pathway for the formation from oxaloacetate of the "aspartate family" of amino acids. As mentioned previously, only plants and microorganisms can synthesize many of these amino acids, most animals requiring such amino acids to be supplied preformed in their diets.

There are a number of pacemaker enzymes in the biosynthetic route for the aspartate family

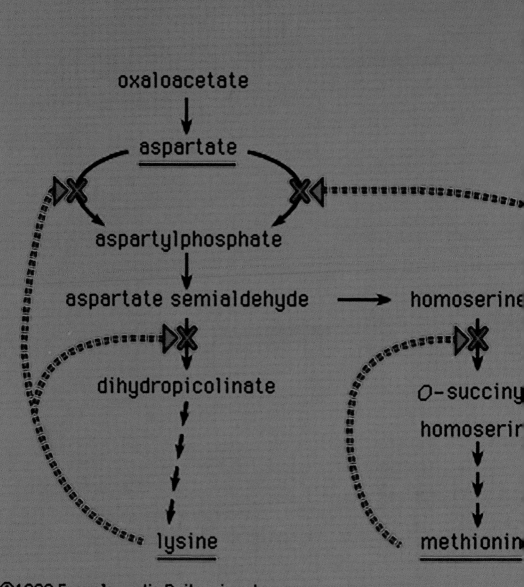

Fine control of the enzymes of the aspartate family in *E. coli*

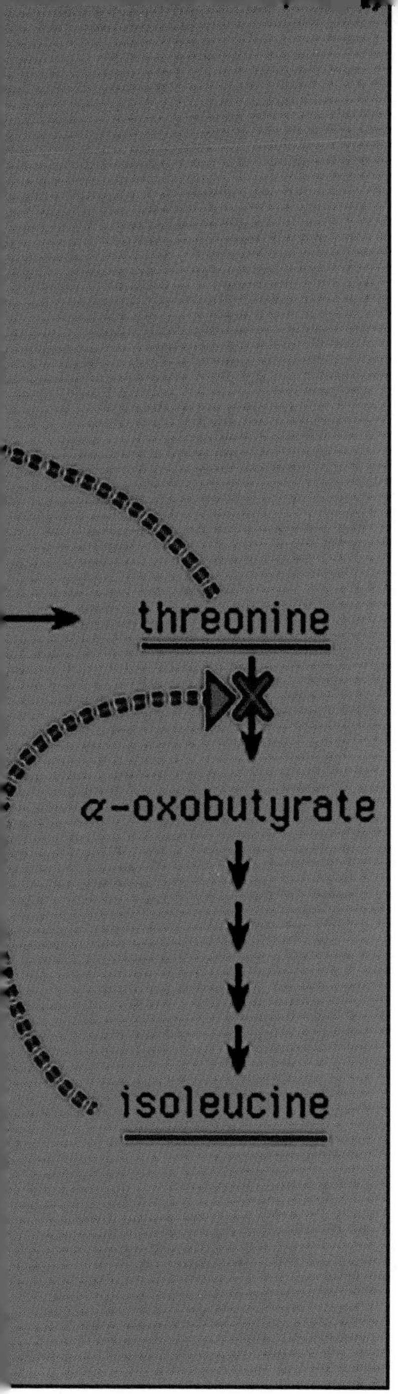

threonine

α-oxobutyrate

isoleucine

of amino acids. Many of these enzymes are uniquely involved in the formation of one product. Each of the enzymes functions after a branch point in the pathway, and all are inhibited specifically by the end product that emerges from the branch point. The supplies of lysine, methionine, and isoleucine required by a cell can be independently regulated. Threonine, however, is both an amino acid essential for protein synthesis and a precursor of isoleucine. If the rate of synthesis of threonine from aspartate were regulated as are the rates of lysine, methionine, and isoleucine, an imbalance in the supply of isoleucine might result. This risk is overcome in *E. coli* by the existence of three different aspartokinase enzymes, all of which catalyze the first step common to the production of all the products derived from aspartate. Each has a different regulatory effector molecule. Thus, one type of aspartokinase is inhibited by lysine, a second by threonine. The third kinase is not inhibited by any naturally occurring amino acid, but its rate of synthesis is controlled by the concentration of methionine within the cell. The triple control mechanism resulting from the three different aspartokinases ensures that the accumulation of one amino acid does not shut off the supply of aspartyl phosphate necessary for the synthesis of the others.

Another example of control through end-product inhibition also illustrates the manner in which the operation of two biosynthetic pathways may be coordinated. Both DNA and the various types of RNA are assembled from purine and pyrimidine nucleotides. These in turn are built up from intermediates of central metabolic pathways. The first step in the synthesis of pyrimidine nucleotides is that catalyzed by aspartate carbamoyltransferase. This step initiates a sequence of reactions that leads to the formation of pyrimidine nucleotides such as UTP and CTP [25]. Studies of aspartate carbamoyltransferase have revealed that the affinity of this enzyme for its substrate (aspartate) is markedly decreased by the presence of CTP. This effect can be overcome by the addition of ATP, a purine nucleotide. The enzyme can be dissociated into two subunits: one contains the enzymatic activity and (in the dissociated form) does not bind CTP; the other binds CTP but has no catalytic activity. Apart from providing physical evidence that pacemaker enzymes contain distinct catalytic and regulatory sites, the interaction of aspartate carbamoyltransferase with the different nucleotides provides an explanation for the control of the supply of nucleic acid precursors. If a cell contains sufficient pyrimidine nucleotides (e.g., UTP), aspartate carbamoyltransferase, the first enzyme of pyrimidine biosynthesis, is inhibited. If, however, the cell contains high levels of purine nucleotides (e.g., ATP), as required for the formation of nucleic acids, the inhibition of aspartate carbamoyltransferase is relieved, and pyrimidines are formed.

Positive Modulation

Not all pacemaker enzymes are controlled by inhibition of their activity. Instead, some are subject to positive modulation—i.e., the effector is required for the efficient functioning of the enzyme. Such enzymes exhibit little activity in the absence of the appropriate allosteric effector. One instance of positive modulation is the anaplerotic fixation of carbon dioxide onto pyruvate and phosphoenolpyruvate (PEP). This example also illustrates how a metabolic product of one route controls the rate of nutrient flow of another.

The carboxylation of pyruvate in higher organisms and the carboxylation of phosphoenolpyruvate in gut bacteria occurs at a significant rate only if acetyl coenzyme A is present. Acetyl coenzyme A acts as a positive allosteric effector and is not broken down in the course of the reaction. Moreover, some pyruvate carboxylases and the PEP carboxylase of gut bacteria are inhibited by four-carbon compounds (e.g., aspartate). These substances inhibit because they interfere with the binding of the positive effector, acetyl coenzyme A. Such enzymatic controls are reasonable in a physiological sense. It will be recalled that anaplerotic formation of oxaloacetate from pyruvate or PEP is required to provide the acceptor for the entry of acetyl coenzyme A into the TCA cycle. The reaction need occur only if acetyl coenzyme A is present in sufficient amounts. On the other hand, an abundance of four-carbon intermediates obviates the necessity for forming more through carboxylation reactions such as [1] and [1a].

Similar reasoning, though in the opposite sense, can be applied to the control of another anaplerotic sequence, the glyoxylate cycle. The biosynthesis of cell materials from the two-carbon compound acetate is, in principle, akin to biosynthesis from TCA cycle intermediates. In both processes, it is the availability of intermediates such as PEP and pyruvate that determines the rate at which a cell forms the many components produced through gluconeogenesis. Although in the strictest sense the glyoxylate cycle has no defined end product, PEP and pyruvate are, for these physiological reasons, best fitted to regulate the rate at which the glyoxylate cycle is required to operate. It is thus not unexpected that the pacemaker enzyme of the glyoxylate cycle, isocitrate lyase, is allosterically inhibited by PEP and by pyruvate.

ENERGY STATE OF THE CELL

It is characteristic of catabolic routes that they do not lead to uniquely identifiable end products. The major products of glycolysis and the TCA cycle, for example, are carbon dioxide and water. Within the cell, the concentrations of both are unlikely to vary sufficiently to allow them to serve as effective regulatory metabolites. The processes by which water is produced initially involve, however, the reduction of coenzymes, the reoxidation of which is accompanied by the synthesis of ATP from ADP. Moreover, the utilization of ATP in energy-consuming reactions yields ADP and AMP. At any given moment, therefore, a living cell contains ATP, ADP, and AMP. The relative proportion of the three nucleotides provides an index of the energy state of the cell. It is thus reasonable that the flux of nutrients through catabolic routes is, in general, impeded by high intracellular levels of both reduced coenzymes (e.g., $FADH_2$, reduced NAD^+) and ATP, and that these inhibitory effects are often overcome by AMP.

The control exerted by the levels of ATP, ADP, and AMP within the cell is illustrated by the regulatory mechanisms of glycolysis and the TCA cycle. These nucleotides also serve to govern the occurrence of the opposite pathway, gluconeogenesis, and to avoid mutual interference of the catabolic and anabolic sequences. Although not all of the controls mentioned have been found to operate in all living organisms examined, it has been observed that, in general:

1. Glucose 6-phosphate stimulates glycogen synthesis from glucose 1-phosphate and inhibits both glycogen breakdown and its own formation from glucose.

2. Phosphofructokinase, the most important pacemaker enzyme of glycolysis, is inhibited by high levels of its own substrates (fructose 6-phosphate and ATP). This inhibition is overcome by AMP. In tissues, such as heart muscle, which use fatty acids as a major fuel, inhibition of glycolysis by citrate may be physiologically the more important means of control. Control by citrate, the first intermediate of the TCA cycle, which produces the bulk of the cellular ATP, is thus the same, in principle, as control through ATP.

3. Fructose 1,6-diphosphatase, which catalyzes the reaction opposite to phosphofructokinase, is strongly inhibited by AMP.

4. Rapid catabolism of carbohydrate requires the efficient conversion of PEP to pyruvate. In liver and in some bacteria the activity of the pyruvate kinase that catalyzes this process is greatly stimulated by the presence of fructose 1,6-diphosphate, which thus acts as a potentiator of a reaction required for its ultimate catabolism.

5. The oxidation of pyruvate to acetyl coenzyme A is inhibited by acetyl coenzyme A. Because acetyl coenzyme A also acts as a positive modulator of pyruvate carboxylation, this control reinforces the partition between pyruvate catabolism and its conversion to four-carbon intermediates for anaplerosis and gluconeogenesis.

6. Citrate synthase, the first enzyme of the TCA cycle, is inhibited by ATP in higher organisms and by reduced NAD^+ in many microorganisms. In some strictly aerobic bacteria, the inhibition by reduced NAD^+ is overcome by AMP.

7. Citrate acts as a positive effector for the first enzyme of fatty acid biosynthesis. A high level

of citrate, which also indicates a sufficient energy supply, thus inhibits carbohydrate fragmentation and diverts the carbohydrate that has been fragmented from combustion to the formation of lipids.

8. Some forms of isocitrate dehydrogenase are maximally active only in the presence of ADP or AMP and are inhibited by ATP. This is an example of regulation by covalent modification of an enzyme since the action of ATP here is to phosphorylate, and consequently to inactivate, the isocitrate dehydrogenase. A specific phosphatase, which is a different enzymatic activity of the protein that effects the phosphorylation by ATP, catalyzes the splitting-off by water of the phosphate moiety on the inactive isocitrate dehydrogenase and thus restricts activity. Again, the energy state of the cell serves as the signal regulating an enzyme involved in energy transduction.

COARSE CONTROL

Although fine control mechanisms allow the sensitive adjustment of the flux of nutrients along metabolic pathways relative to the needs of cells under relatively constant environmental conditions, these processes may not be adequate to cope with severe changes in the chemical milieu. Such severe changes may arise in higher organisms with a change in diet or when, in response to other stimuli, the hormonal balance is altered. In starvation, for example, the overriding need to maintain blood glucose levels may require the liver to synthesize glucose from noncarbohydrate products of tissue breakdown at rates greater than can be achieved by the enzymes normally present in the liver. Under such circumstances, cellular concentrations of key enzymes of gluconeogenesis, such as pyruvate carboxylase and PEP carboxykinase, may rise by as much as 10-fold, while the concentration of glucokinase and of the enzymes of fatty acid synthesis decreases to a similar extent. Conversely, high carbohydrate diets and administration of the hormone insulin to diabetic animals elicit a preferential synthesis of glucokinase and pyruvate kinase. These changes in the relative proportions and absolute amounts of key enzymes are the net result of increases in the rate of their synthesis and decreases in the rate of their destruction. Although such changes reflect changes in the rates of either transcription, translation, or both of specific regions of the genome, the mechanisms by which the changes are effected have not yet been clarified.

Microorganisms sometimes encounter changes in environment much more severe than those encountered by the cells of tissues and organs, and their responses are correspondingly greater.

Mention has already been made of the ability of *E. coli* to form β-galactosidase when transferred to a medium containing lactose as the sole carbon source. Such a transfer may result in an increase of 1,000-fold or more in the cellular concentration of the enzyme. Because this preferential enzyme synthesis is elicited by exposure of the cells to lactose, or to non-metabolizable but chemically similar analogues, and because synthesis ceases as soon as the eliciting agents (inducers) are removed, β-galactosidase is called an inducible enzyme. It has been established that a regulator gene exists that specifies the amino-acid sequence of a so-called repressor protein, and that the repressor protein binds to a unique portion of the region of DNA concerned with β-galactosidase formation. Under these circumstances the DNA is not transcribed to mRNA, and virtually no enzyme is made. The repressor, however, is an allosteric protein and readily combines with inducers. Such a combination prevents the repressor from binding to DNA and allows transcription and translation of β-galactosidase to proceed.

Although this mechanism for the specific control of gene activity may not apply to the regulation of all inducible enzymes—for example, those concerned with the utilization of the sugar arabinose—and is not universally applicable to all coarse control processes in all microorganisms, it can explain the manner in which the presence in growth media of at least some cell components represses (i.e., inhibits the synthesis of) enzymes normally involved in the formation of such components by gut bacteria such as *E. coli.* Although, for example, the bacteria must obviously make amino acids from ammonia if that is the sole source of nitrogen available to them, it would not be necessary for the bacteria to synthesize enzymes required for the formation of amino acids supplied preformed in the medium. Thus, of the three aspartokinases formed by *E. coli*, two are repressed by their end products, methionine and lysine. On the other hand, the third aspartokinase, which is inhibited by threonine, is repressed by threonine only if isoleucine is also present. This example of so-called multivalent repression is of obvious physiological utility. It is likely that the amino acids that thus specifically inhibit the synthesis of aspartokinases do so by combining with specific protein repressor molecules. However, whereas the combination of the inducer with the repressor of β-galactosidase inactivates the repressor protein and hence permits synthesis of the enzyme, the repressor proteins for biosynthetic enzymes would not bind to DNA unless they were also combined with the appropriate amino acid. Aspartokinase synthesis would thus occur in the absence of the end-product effectors and not in their presence.

This explanation applies also to the coarse control of the anaplerotic glyoxylate cycle. The synthesis of both of the enzymes unique to that cycle, isocitrate lyase and malate synthase, is controlled by a regulator gene that presumably specifies a repressor protein unable to bind to DNA unless combined with pyruvate or PEP. Cells growing on acetate do not contain high levels of these intermediates because they are continuously being removed for biosynthesis. The enzymes of the glyoxylate cycle are therefore formed at high rates. If pyruvate or substances catabolized to PEP or pyruvate are added to the medium, however, further synthesis of the two enzymes is speedily repressed.

CHAPTER
6

PHOTOSYNTHESIS

P hotosynthesis, the process by which green plants and certain other organisms transform light energy into chemical energy, is another chemical reaction of metabolism. During photosynthesis in green plants, light energy is captured and used to convert water, carbon dioxide, and minerals into oxygen and energy-rich organic compounds. It would be impossible to overestimate the importance of photosynthesis in the maintenance of life on Earth. If photosynthesis ceased, there would soon be little food or other organic matter on Earth. Most organisms would disappear, and in time Earth's atmosphere would become nearly devoid of gaseous oxygen. The only organisms able to exist under such conditions would be the chemosynthetic bacteria, which can utilize the chemical energy of certain inorganic compounds and thus are not dependent on the conversion of light energy.

Photosynthesis also is responsible for the "fossil fuels" (i.e., coal, oil, and gas) that power industrial society. In past ages, green plants and small organisms that fed on plants increased faster than they were consumed, and their remains were deposited in Earth's crust by sedimentation and other geological processes. There, protected from oxidation, these organic remains were slowly converted to fossil fuels. These fuels not only provide much of the energy used in factories, homes, and transportation, but they also serve as the raw material for plastics and other synthetic products. Unfortunately, modern civilization is using up in a few centuries the excess of photosynthetic production accumulated over millions of years.

Modern power plants use up more energy than plants can produce through photosynthesis.

Requirements for food, materials, and energy in a world where human population is rapidly growing have created a need to increase both the amount of photosynthesis and the efficiency of converting photosynthetic output into products useful to people. One response to these needs—the so-called "Green Revolution"—has achieved enormous improvements in agricultural yield through the use of chemical fertilizers, pest and plant disease control, plant breeding, and mechanized tilling, harvesting, and crop processing. This effort has limited severe famines to a few areas of the world despite rapid population growth, but it has not eliminated widespread malnutrition.

A second agricultural revolution, based on plant genetic engineering, may lead to increases in plant productivity and thereby partially alleviate malnutrition. Since the 1970s molecular biologists have possessed the means to manipulate a plant's genetic material (DNA) to achieve improvements in disease and drought resistance, product yield and quality, frost hardiness, and other desirable properties. In the future, such genetic engineering may result in improvements in the process of photosynthesis.

EARLY OBSERVATIONS

The study of photosynthesis began in 1771, with observations made by the English chemist Joseph Priestley. Priestley had burned a candle in a closed container until the air within the container could no longer support combustion. He then placed a sprig of mint plant in the container and discovered that after several days the mint had produced some substance (later recognized as oxygen) that enabled the confined air to again support combustion. In 1779 the Dutch physician Jan Ingenhousz expanded upon Priestley's work, showing that the plant must be exposed to light if the combustible substance (i.e., oxygen) was to be restored. He also demonstrated that this process required the presence of the green tissues of the plant, and that all living parts of the plant "damage" the air (respire), with the extent of air restoration by a green plant far exceeding its damaging effect.

In 1782 it was demonstrated that the combustion supporting gas (oxygen) was formed at the expense of another gas, or "fixed air," which had been identified the year before as carbon dioxide. Gas-exchange experiments in 1804 showed that the gain in weight of a plant grown in a carefully weighed pot was the sum of carbon, which came entirely from absorbed carbon dioxide, and water taken up by plant roots. Almost half a century passed before the concept of chemical energy developed sufficiently to permit the discovery (in 1845) that light energy from the sun is stored as chemical energy in products formed during photosynthesis.

OVERALL REACTION

In chemical terms, photosynthesis is a light-energized oxidation-reduction process. (Oxidation refers to the removal of electrons from a molecule; reduction refers to the gain of electrons by a molecule.) In plant photosynthesis, the energy of light is used to drive the oxidation of water (H_2O), producing oxygen gas (O_2), hydrogen ions (H^+), and electrons. Most of the removed electrons and hydrogen ions ultimately are transferred to carbon dioxide (CO_2), which is reduced to organic products. Other electrons and hydrogen ions are used to reduce nitrate and sulfate to amino and sulfhydryl groups in amino acids, which are the building blocks of proteins. In most green cells, carbohydrates—especially starch and the sugar sucrose—are the major direct organic products of photosynthesis. The overall reaction in which carbohydrates—represented by the general formula (CH_2O)—are formed during plant photosynthesis can be indicated by the following equation:

$$CO_2 + 2H_2O \quad \xrightarrow[\text{green plants}]{\text{light}} \quad (CH_2O) + O_2 + H_2O$$

This equation is merely a summary statement, for the process of photosynthesis actually involves numerous complex reactions. These reactions occur

239

in two stages: the "light" stage, consisting of photochemical (i.e., light-dependent) reactions; and the
"dark" stage, comprising chemical reactions controlled by enzymes (organic catalysts). During the
first stage, the energy of light is absorbed and used
to drive a series of electron transfers, resulting in the
synthesis of the energy-rich compound ATP and the
electron donor reduced nicotine adenine dinucleotide phosphate (NADPH). During the dark stage, the
ATP and NADPH formed in the light reactions are
used to reduce carbon dioxide to organic carbon
compounds. This assimilation of inorganic carbon
into organic compounds is called carbon fixation.

　During the 20th century, comparisons between
photosynthetic processes in green plants and in
certain photosynthetic sulfur bacteria provided
important information about the photosynthetic
mechanism. Sulfur bacteria use hydrogen sulfide
(H_2S) as a source of hydrogen atoms and produce
sulfur instead of oxygen during photosynthesis. The
overall reaction is:

$$CO_2 + 2H_2S \xrightarrow[\text{sulfur bacteria}]{\text{light}} (CH_2O) + S_2 + H_2O$$

　In the 1930s Dutch biologist Cornelis van Niel
recognized that the utilization of carbon dioxide to
form organic compounds was similar in the two

types of photosynthetic organisms. Suggesting that differences existed in the light-dependent stage and in the nature of the compounds used as a source of hydrogen atoms, he proposed that hydrogen was transferred from hydrogen sulfide (in bacteria) or water (in green plants) to an unknown acceptor (called A), which was reduced to H_2A. During the dark reactions, which are similar in both bacteria and green plants, the reduced acceptor (H_2A) reacted with carbon dioxide (CO_2) to form carbohydrate (CH_2O) and to oxidize the unknown acceptor to A. This putative reaction can be represented as:

$$CO_2 + 2H_2A \xrightarrow{\text{light}} (CH_2O) + 2A + H_2O$$

Van Niel's proposal was important because the popular (but incorrect) theory had been that oxygen was removed from carbon dioxide (rather than hydrogen from water) and that carbon then combined with water to form carbohydrate (rather than the hydrogen from water combining with CO_2 to form CH_2O).

By 1940 chemists were using heavy isotopes to follow the reactions of photosynthesis. Water marked with an isotope of oxygen (^{18}O) was used in early experiments. Plants that photosynthesized in the presence of water containing $H_2^{18}O$ produced oxygen gas containing ^{18}O. Those that photosynthesized in the presence of normal water produced normal oxygen gas. These results provided strong support for van Niel's theory that the oxygen gas produced during photosynthesis is derived from water.

PRODUCTS OF PHOTOSYNTHESIS

As has been stated, carbohydrates are the most important direct organic product of photosynthesis in the majority of green plants. The formation of a simple carbohydrate, glucose, is indicated by a chemical equation,

$$6CO_2 + 12H_2S \xrightarrow[\text{green plants}]{\text{light}} C_2H_{12}O_6 + 6O_2 + 6H_2O$$

carbon dioxide   water   glucose   oxygen   water

Little free glucose is produced in plants. Instead, glucose units are linked together to form starch or are joined with fructose, another sugar, to form sucrose. Not only carbohydrates, as was once thought, but also amino acids, proteins, lipids (or fats), pigments, and other organic components of green tissues are synthesized during photosynthesis. Minerals supply the elements (e.g., nitrogen, N; phosphorus, P; sulfur, S) required to form these compounds. Chemical bonds are broken between oxygen (O) and carbon (C), hydrogen (H), nitrogen, and sulfur, and new bonds are formed in products that include gaseous oxygen (O_2) and organic compounds. More energy is required to break the bonds between oxygen and other elements (e.g., in water, nitrate, and sulfate) than is released when new bonds form in the products. This difference in bond energy accounts for a large part of the light energy stored as chemical energy in the organic products formed during photosynthesis. Additional energy is stored in making complex molecules from simple ones.

EVOLUTION OF PHOTOSYNTHESIS

Although life and the quality of the atmosphere today depend on photosynthesis, it is likely that green plants evolved long after the first living cells. When Earth was young, electrical storms and solar radiation probably provided the energy for the synthesis of complex molecules from abundant simpler ones, such as water, ammonia, and methane. The first living cells probably evolved from these complex molecules. For example, the accidental joining together (condensation) of the amino acid glycine and the fatty acid acetate may have formed complex organic molecules known as porphyrins. These molecules, in turn, may have evolved further into coloured molecules called pigments—e.g., chlorophylls of green plants, bacteriochlorophyll of photosynthetic bacteria, hemin (the red pigment of blood), and cytochromes, a group of pigment molecules essential in both photosynthesis and cellular respiration.

Primitive coloured cells then had to evolve mechanisms for using the light energy absorbed by their pigments. At first, the energy may have been used immediately to initiate reactions useful to the cell. As the process for utilization of light energy continued to evolve, however, a larger part of the absorbed light energy probably was stored as chemical energy, to be used to maintain life. Green plants, with their ability to use light energy to convert carbon dioxide and water to carbohydrates and oxygen, are the culmination of this evolutionary process.

The first oxygenic (oxygen-producing) cells probably were the cyanophytes, or "blue-green algae," which appeared about 2 billion to 3 billion years ago. These microscopic organisms are believed to have greatly increased the oxygen content of the atmosphere, making possible the development of aerobic (oxygen-using) organisms. Cyanophytes are prokaryotic cells—they contain no distinct, membrane-enclosed subcellular particles (organelles), such as nuclei and chloroplasts. Green plants, by contrast, are composed of eukaryotic cells, in which the photosynthetic apparatus is contained within membrane-bound chloroplasts. There is a theory that the first photosynthetic eukaryotes were red algae that may have developed when nonphotosynthetic eukaryotic cells engulfed cyanophytes. Within the host cells, these cyanophytes are thought to have evolved into chloroplasts. Alternatively, the ancestors of chloroplasts in green plants may have been another oxygenic prokaryote like *Prochloron*, an organism that has been found only growing symbiotically inside ascidians.

There are a number of photosynthetic bacteria that are not oxygenic (e.g., the sulfur bacteria previously discussed). The evolutionary pathway that led to these bacteria diverged from the one that resulted in oxygenic organisms. In addition to the absence of oxygen production, nonoxygenic photosynthesis differs from oxygenic photosynthesis in two other ways: light of longer wavelengths is absorbed and used by pigments called bacteriochlorophylls, and reduced compounds other than water (such as hydrogen sulfide or organic molecules) provide the electrons needed for the reduction of carbon dioxide.

FACTORS THAT INFLUENCE RATE

The rate of photosynthesis is defined in terms of the rate of oxygen production either per unit mass (or area) of green plant tissues or per unit weight of total chlorophyll. The amount of light, the carbon dioxide supply, the temperature, the water supply, and the availability of minerals are the most important environmental factors that directly affect the rate of photosynthesis in land plants. The rate of photosynthesis also is determined by the plant species and its physiological state—e.g., its health, its maturity, and whether or not it is in flower.

LIGHT INTENSITY AND TEMPERATURE

As has been mentioned, the complex mechanism of photosynthesis includes a photochemical, or light-dependent, stage and an enzymatic, or dark, stage that involves chemical reactions. These stages can be distinguished by studying the rates of photosynthesis at various degrees of light saturation (i.e., intensity) and at different temperatures. Over a range of moderate temperatures and at low to medium light intensities (relative to the normal range of the plant species), the rate of photosynthesis increases as the intensity increases and is independent of temperature. As the light intensity increases to higher levels, however, the rate becomes increasingly dependent on temperature and less dependent on intensity. Light "saturation" is achieved at a specific light intensity, and the rate then is dependent only on temperature if all other factors are constant. In the light-dependent range before saturation, therefore, the rate of photosynthesis is determined by the rates of photochemical steps. At high light intensities, some of the chemical reactions of the dark stage become rate-limiting. At light saturation, rate increases with temperature until a point is reached beyond which no further rate increase can occur. In many land plants, moreover, a process called photorespiration occurs at high light intensities and temperatures. Photorespiration competes with photosynthesis and limits further increases in the rate of photosynthesis, especially if the supply of water is limited.

CARBON DIOXIDE

Included among the rate-limiting steps of the dark stage of photosynthesis are the chemical reactions by which organic compounds are formed using carbon dioxide as a carbon source. The rates of these reactions can be increased somewhat by increasing the carbon dioxide concentration. During the 19th and 20th centuries, the level of carbon dioxide in the atmosphere has been rising due to the extensive combustion of fossil fuels. The atmospheric level of carbon dioxide climbed from about 0.028 percent (228 parts per million, or ppm) in 1860 to 0.0315 percent (315 ppm) by 1958 (when improved measurements began), and to 0.034 percent (340 ppm) by 1981 and 0.039 percent (390 ppm) by 2010. This increase in carbon dioxide directly increases plant photosynthesis, but the size of the increase depends on the species and physiological condition of the plant. Furthermore, increasing levels of atmospheric carbon dioxide result in climatic changes, including increased global temperatures, which can affect photosynthesis rates.

WATER

For land plants, water availability can function as a limiting factor in photosynthesis and plant growth. Besides the requirement for water in the photosynthetic reaction itself, water is transpired from the leaves—it

In autumn chlorophyll production slows as the days get shorter and cooler. As the remaining chlorophyll breaks down and fades, the colours of other pigments are revealed, producing the colourful foliage seen here.

evaporates from the leaves to the atmosphere via the stomates. These stomates are small openings through the leaf epidermis, or outer skin. They permit the entry of carbon dioxide but also allow the exit of water vapour. The stomates open and close according to the physiological needs of the leaf. In hot and arid climates the stomates may close to conserve water, but this closure limits the entry of carbon dioxide and hence the rate of photosynthesis, while the wasteful process of photorespiration may increase. If the level of carbon dioxide in the atmosphere increases, more carbon dioxide could enter through a smaller opening of the stomates, so that more photosynthesis could occur with a given supply of water.

MINERALS

Several minerals are required for healthy plant growth and for maximum rates of photosynthesis. Nitrate or ammonia, sulfate, phosphate, iron, magnesium, and potassium are required in substantial amounts for the synthesis of amino acids, proteins, coenzymes, DNA and RNA, chlorophyll and other pigments, and other essential plant constituents. Smaller amounts of such elements as manganese, copper, and chlorine are required in photosynthesis. Some other trace elements are needed for various nonphotosynthetic functions in plants.

INTERNAL FACTORS

Each plant species adapts to a range of environmental factors. Within this normal range of conditions, complex regulatory mechanisms in the plant's cells adjust the activities of enzymes (i.e., organic catalysts). These adjustments maintain a balance in the overall photosynthetic process and control it in accordance with the needs of the whole plant. With a given plant species, for example, doubling the carbon dioxide level might cause a temporary increase of nearly twofold in the rate of photosynthesis. A few hours later, however, the rate might fall to the original level because photosynthesis had made more sucrose than the rest of the plant could use. By contrast, another plant species provided with such carbon dioxide enrichment might be able to use more sucrose and would continue to photosynthesize and to grow faster throughout most of its life cycle.

ENERGY EFFICIENCY

The energy efficiency of photosynthesis is the ratio of the energy stored to the energy of light absorbed. The chemical energy stored is the difference between that contained in gaseous oxygen and organic compound products and the energy of water, carbon dioxide, and other reactants. The amount of energy stored can be estimated only because many products are formed, and these vary with the plant species and environmental conditions. If the equation for glucose formation given earlier is used to approximate the actual storage process, the production of one mole (i.e., 6.02×10^{23} molecules; abbreviated N) of oxygen and one-sixth mole of glucose results in the storage of about 117 kilocalories (kcal) of chemical energy. This amount must then be compared to the energy of light absorbed to produce one mole of oxygen in order to calculate the efficiency of photosynthesis.

Light can be described as a wave of particles known as photons. These are units of energy, or light quanta. The quantity N photons is called an einstein. The energy of light varies inversely with the length of the photon waves. In other words, the shorter the wavelength, the greater the energy content. The energy (e) of a photon is given by the equation $e = h\, c/\lambda$, where c is the velocity of light, h is Planck's constant, and λ is the light wavelength. The energy (E) of an einstein is $E = N e = N h\, c/\lambda = 28{,}600/\lambda$, when E is in kilocalories and λ is given in nanometres (nm; 1 nm $= 10^{-9}$ metres). An einstein of red light with a wavelength of 680 nm has an energy of about 42 kcal. Blue light has a shorter wavelength and therefore more energy than red light. Regardless of whether the light is blue or red, however, the same number of einsteins are required for photosynthesis per mole of oxygen formed. The part of the solar spectrum used by plants has an estimated mean wavelength of 570 nanometres. Therefore, the energy of light used during photosynthesis is approximately 28,600/570, or 50 kilocalories per einstein.

In order to compute the amount of light energy involved in photosynthesis, one other value is needed: the number of einsteins absorbed per mole of oxygen evolved. This is called the quantum requirement. The minimum quantum requirement for photosynthesis under optimal conditions is about nine. Thus the energy used is 9 × 50, or 450 kilocalories per mole of oxygen evolved. Therefore, the estimated maximum energy efficiency of photosynthesis is the energy stored per mole of oxygen evolved—117 kilocalories—divided by 450; that is, 117/450, or 26 percent.

The actual percentage of solar energy stored by plants is much less than the maximum energy efficiency of photosynthesis. An agricultural crop in which the biomass (total dry weight) stores as much as 1 percent of total solar energy received on an annual area-wide basis is exceptional, although a few cases of higher yields (perhaps as much as 3.5 percent in sugarcane) are reported. There are several reasons for this difference between the predicted maximum efficiency of photosynthesis and the actual energy stored in biomass. First, more than half of the incident sunlight is composed of wavelengths too long to be absorbed, while some of the remainder is reflected or lost to the leaves. Consequently, plants can at best absorb only about 34 percent of the incident sunlight. Second, plants must carry out a variety of physiological processes in such non-photosynthetic tissues as roots and stems. These processes, as well as cellular respiration in all parts of the plant, use up stored energy. Third, rates of photosynthesis in bright sunlight sometimes exceed the needs of the plants, resulting in the formation of excess sugars and starch. When this happens, the regulatory mechanisms of the plant slow down the process of photosynthesis, allowing more absorbed sunlight to go unused. Fourth, in many plants, energy is wasted by the process of photorespiration. Finally, the growing season may last only a few months of the year. Sunlight received during other seasons is not used. Furthermore, it should be noted that if only agricultural products (e.g., seeds, fruits, and tubers, rather than total biomass) are considered as the end product of the energy conversion process of photo-synthesis, the efficiency falls even further.

CHLOROPLASTS

The process of plant photosynthesis takes place entirely within the chloroplasts. Detailed studies of the role of these organelles date from the work of the British biochemist Robert Hill. About 1940 Hill discovered that green particles obtained from broken cells could produce oxygen from water in the presence of light and a chemical compound, such as ferric oxalate, able to serve as an electron acceptor. This process is known as the Hill reaction. During the 1950s Daniel Arnon and other American biochemists prepared plant cell fragments in which not only the Hill reaction but also the synthesis of the energy-storage compound ATP occurred. In addition, the coenzyme NADP was used as the final acceptor of electrons, replacing the nonphysiological electron acceptors used by Hill. His procedures were refined further so that individual small pieces of isolated chloroplast membranes, or lamellae, could perform the Hill reaction. These small pieces of lamellae were then fragmented into pieces so small that they performed only the light reactions of the photosynthetic process. It is now possible also to isolate the entire chloroplast so that it can carry out the complete process of photosynthesis, from light absorption, oxygen formation, and the reduction of carbon dioxide to the formation of glucose and other products.

STRUCTURAL FEATURES

The intricate structural organization of the photosynthetic apparatus is essential for the efficient performance of the complex process of photosynthesis. The chloroplast is enclosed in a double outer membrane, and its size approximates a spheroid about 2,500 nanometres thick and 5,000 nanometres long. Some single-celled algae have one chloroplast that occupies more than half the cell volume. Leaf

Chloroplast

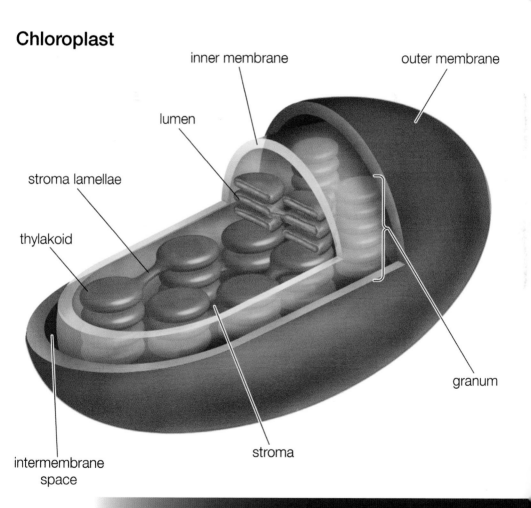

inner membrane

outer membrane

lumen

stroma lamellae

thylakoid

granum

intermembrane space

stroma

The internal (thylakoid) membrane vesicles of a chloroplast are organized into stacks, which reside in a matrix known as the stroma. All the chlorophyll in the chloroplast is contained in the membranes of the thylakoid vesicles.

cells of higher plants contain many chloroplasts, each approximately the size of the one in some algal cells. When thin sections of a chloroplast are examined under the electron microscope, several features are apparent. Chief among these are the intricate internal membranes (i.e., the lamellae) and the stroma, a colourless matrix in which the lamellae are embedded. Also visible are starch granules, which appear as dense bodies. The stroma is basically a solution of enzymes and small molecules. The dark reactions occur in the stroma, the soluble enzymes of which catalyze the conversion of carbon dioxide and minerals to carbohydrates and other organic compounds. The capacity for carbon fixation and reduction is lost if the outer membrane of the chloroplast is broken, allowing the stroma enzymes to leak out.

Asingle lamella, which contains all the photosynthetic pigments, is approximately 10–15 nanometres thick. The lamellae exist in more-or-less flat sheets, a few of which extend through much of the length of the chloroplast. Examination of cross sections of lamellae under the electron microscope shows that their edges are joined to form closed hollow disks that are called thylakoids ("saclike"). The chloroplasts of most higher plants have regions, called grana, in which the thylakoids are very tightly stacked. When viewed by electron microscopy at an oblique angle, the grana appear as stacks of disks. When viewed in cross section, it is apparent that some thylakoids extend from one grana through the stroma into other grana. The thin aqueous spaces inside the thylakoids are believed to be connected with each other via these stroma thylakoids. These thylakoid spaces are isolated from the stroma spaces by the relatively impermeable lamellae.

The light reactions occur exclusively in the thylakoids. The complex structural organization of lamellae is required for proper thylakoid function. Intact thylakoids apparently are necessary for the formation of ATP. Thylakoids that have been broken down to smaller units can no longer form ATP, even when the conversion of light into chemical energy occurs during electron transport in these units. Such lamellar fragments can carry out the Hill reaction, with the transfer of electrons from water to $NADP^+$.

LAMELLAE

Lamellae consist of about equal amounts of lipids and proteins. About one-fourth of the lipid portion of the lamellae consists of pigments and coenzymes. The remainder of the lamellae consists of various lipids, including polar compounds such as phospholipids and galactolipids. These polar lipid molecules have "head" groups that attract water (i.e., are hydrophilic) and fatty acid "tails" that are oil soluble and repel water (i.e., are hydrophobic). When polar lipids are placed in an aqueous environment, they can line up with the fatty acid tails side by side. A second layer of phospholipids forms tail-to-tail with the first, establishing a lipid bilayer in which the hydrophilic heads are in contact with the aqueous solution on each side of the bilayer. Sandwiched between the heads are the hydrophobic tails, creating a hydrophobic environment from which water is excluded. This lipid bilayer is an essential feature of all biological membranes. The hydrophobic parts of proteins and lipid-soluble cofactors and pigments are dissolved or embedded in the lipid bilayer. Lamellar membranes can function as electrical insulating material and permit a charge, or potential difference, to develop across the membrane. Such a charge can be a source of chemical or electrical energy.

LIPIDS

Approximately one-fifth of the lamellar lipids are chlorophyll molecules. One type, chlorophyll *a*, is more abundant than the second type, chlorophyll *b*. The chlorophyll molecules are specifically bound to small protein molecules. Most of these chlorophyll-proteins are "light-harvesting" pigments. These absorb light and pass its energy on to special chlorophyll *a* molecules that are directly involved in the conversion of light energy to chemical energy. When one of these special chlorophyll *a* molecules is excited by light energy, it gives up an electron. There are two types of these special chlorophyll a molecules: one, called P_{680}, has an absorption spectrum that peaks at 684 nanometres; the other, called P_{700}, shows an absorption peak at 700 nanometres.

Although chlorophylls are the main light-absorbing molecules in green plants, other pigments such as carotenes and carotenoids (which are responsible for the yellow-orange colour of carrots) also can absorb light and may supplement chlorophyll as the light-absorbing molecules in some plant cells. The light energy absorbed by these pigments must be passed to chlorophyll before conversion to chemical energy can occur.

Proteins

Many of the lamellar proteins are components of the chlorophyll-protein complexes previously described. Other proteins include enzymes and protein-containing coenzymes. Enzymes are required as organic catalysts for specific reactions within the lamellae. Protein coenzymes, also called cofactors, include important electron carrier molecules called cytochromes, which are iron-containing pigments with the pigment portions attached to protein molecules. During electron transfer, an electron is accepted by an iron atom in the pigment portion of a cytochrome molecule, which thus is reduced. Then the electron is transferred to the iron atom in the next cytochrome carrier in the electron transfer chain, thus oxidizing the first cytochrome and reducing the next one in the chain.

In addition to the metal atoms found in the pigment portions of cytochrome molecules, metal atoms also are found in other protein molecules of the lamellae. In proteins with a total molecular weight of 900,000 (based on the weight of hydrogen as one), there are two atoms of manganese, 10 atoms

COENZYMES

Coenzymes are freely diffusing organic compounds that function as cofactors with enzymes in promoting a variety of metabolic reactions. Coenzymes participate in enzyme-mediated catalysis in stoichiometric (mole-for-mole) amounts, are modified during the reaction, and may require another enzyme-catalyzed reaction to restore them to their original state. Examples include nicotinamide adenine dinucleotide (NAD), which accepts hydrogen (and gives it up in another reaction), and ATP, which gives up phosphate groups while transferring chemical energy (and reacquires phosphate in another reaction). Most of the B vitamins are coenzymes and are essential in facilitating the transfer of atoms or groups of atoms between molecules in the formation of carbohydrates, fats, and proteins.

of iron, and six atoms of copper. These metal atoms are required for the catalytic activity of some of the enzymes important in photosynthesis. The manganese atoms are involved in water-splitting and oxygen formation. Both copper- and iron-containing proteins function in electron transport between water and the final electron-acceptor molecule of the light stage of photosynthesis, an iron-containing protein called ferredoxin. Ferredoxin is a soluble component in the chloroplasts. In its reduced form, it gives electrons directly to the systems that reduce nitrate and sulfate and via NADPH to the system that reduces carbon dioxide. A copper-containing protein called plastocyanin (PC) carries electrons at one point in the electron transport chain. PC molecules are water soluble and can move through the inner space of the thylakoids, carrying electrons from one place to another.

QUINONES

Small molecules called plastoquinones are found in substantial numbers in the lamellae. Like the cytochromes, quinones have important roles in carrying electrons between the components of the light reactions. Since they are lipid soluble, they can diffuse through the membrane. They can carry one or two electrons and, in their reduced form (with added electrons), they carry hydrogen atoms that can be released as hydrogen ions when the added electrons are passed on, for example, to a cytochrome.

THE LIGHT REACTIONS

Photosynthesis consists of a number of photo-chemical and enzymatic reactions and occurs in two stages. During the light-dependent stage, chlorophyll absorbs light energy, which excites some electrons in the pigment molecules to higher energy levels. These electrons leave the chloro-phyll and pass along a series of molecules, gen-erating formation of NADPH and high-energy ATP molecules. Oxygen, released as a by-product, passes into the atmosphere through pores in the leaves. NADPH and ATP drive the second stage, the dark reaction (or Calvin cycle, discovered by Melvin Calvin), which does not require light. During this stage glucose is generated using atmospheric carbon dioxide.

The process of photosynthesis begins with the light reaction. The consequence of molecules' absorbing light is the creation of transient excited states whose chemical and physical properties dif-fer greatly from the original molecules. Following light absorption and the excitation of chlorophyll molecules, electrons are transferred along pigment molecules until they reach quinone. This process of electron transfer, similar to that occurring in mitochondria, ultimately results in the conversion of light energy to ATP.

LIGHT ABSORPTION AND ENERGY TRANSFER

The light energy absorbed by a chlorophyll molecule excites some electrons within the structure of the molecule to higher energy levels, or excited states. Light of shorter wavelength (such as blue) has more energy than light of longer wavelength (such as red), so that absorption of blue light creates an excited state of higher energy. A molecule raised to this higher energy state quickly gives up the "extra" energy as heat and falls to its lowest excited state. This lowest excited state is similar to that of a molecule that has just absorbed the longest wavelength light capable of exciting it. In the case of chlorophyll *a*, this lowest excited state corresponds to that of a molecule that has absorbed red light of about 680 nanometres.

The return of *a* chlorophyll a molecule from its lowest excited state to its original low-energy state (ground state) requires the release of the extra energy of the excited state. This can occur in one of several ways. In photosynthesis, most of this energy is conserved as chemical energy by the transfer of an electron from a special chlorophyll a molecule (P_{680} or P_{700}) to an electron acceptor. When this electron transfer is blocked by inhibitors, such

FLUORESCENCE

Fluorescence is the emission of electromagnetic radiation, usually visible light, caused by excitation of atoms in a material, which then reemit almost immediately (within about 10–8 seconds). The initial excitation is usually caused by absorption of energy from incident radiation or particles, such as X-rays or electrons. Because reemission occurs so quickly, the fluorescence ceases as soon as the exciting source is removed, unlike phosphorescence, which persists as an afterglow. A fluorescent lightbulb is coated on the inside with a powder and contains a gas; electricity causes the gas to emit ultraviolet radiation, which then stimulates the tube coating to emit light. The pixels of a television or computer screen fluoresce when electrons from an electron gun strike them. Fluorescence is often used to analyze molecules, and the addition of a fluorescing agent with emissions in the blue region of the spectrum to detergents causes fabrics to appear whiter in sunlight. X-ray fluorescence is used to analyze minerals.

as the herbicide dichlorophenylmethylurea (DCMU), or by low temperature, the energy can be released as red light. Such re-emission of light is called fluorescence. The examination of fluorescence from photosynthetic material in which electron transfer has been blocked has proved to be a useful tool for scientists studying the light reactions.

PATHWAY OF ELECTRONS

The general features of a widely accepted mechanism for photoelectron transfer, in which two light reactions occur during the transfer of electrons from water to carbon dioxide, were proposed by Robert Hill and Fay Bendall in 1960. On a vertical scale representing the relative potential (in volts) of various cofactors of the electrontransfer chain to be oxidized or reduced,

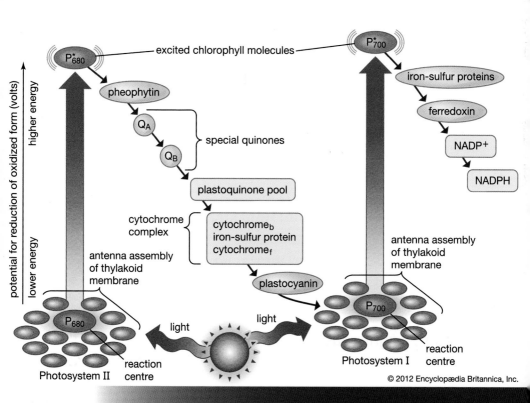

Flow of electrons during the light reaction stage of photosynthesis. Arrows pointing upward represent light reactions that increase the chemical potential; arrows slanting downward represent flow of electrons via carriers in the membrane.

molecules that in their oxidized form have the strongest affinity for electrons (i.e., are strong oxidizing agents) are near the bottom of the scale. Molecules that in their oxidized form are difficult to reduce are near the top of the scale. Once they have accepted electrons, these molecules are strong reducing agents.

In diagrams that describe the light reaction stage of photosynthesis, the actual photochemical steps are indicated by the two vertical arrows, which signify that the special pigments P_{680} and P_{700} receive light energy from the light-harvesting chlorophyll-protein molecules and are raised in energy from their ground state to excited states, symbolized as P^*_{680} and P^*_{700}. In their excited state, these pigments are extremely strong reducing agents that quickly transfer electrons to the first acceptor. These first acceptors also are strong reducing agents and rapidly pass electrons to more stable carriers. In light reaction II the first acceptor may be pheophytin (Ph; a molecule similar to chlorophyll), which also has a strong reducing potential and quickly transfers electrons to the next acceptor. Q_A and Q_B are special quinones, similar to plastoquinone. They receive electrons from pheophytin and pass them to the intermediate electron carriers, which include the plastoquinone (PQ) pool and the cytochromes b and f (Cyt_b and Cyt_f) associated in a complex with an iron-sulfur protein (Fe-S). In light reaction I the identity of the first electron acceptor, X, is not known. It passes electrons on to ironsulfur proteins (Fe-S-protein) in the lamellar membrane, after which the electrons flow to ferredoxin (Fd), a small, water-soluble iron-sulfur protein. When $NADP^+$ and a suitable enzyme are present, two ferredoxin molecules, carrying one electron each, transfer two electrons to $NADP^+$, which picks up a proton (i.e., a hydrogen ion) and becomes NADPH.

Each time a P_{680} or P_{700} molecule gives up an electron, it returns to its ground (unexcited) state, but with a positive charge due to the loss of the electron. These positively charged ions are extremely strong oxidizing agents that remove an electron from a suitable donor. The P^+ of 680 light reaction II is capable of taking electrons from water in the presence of appropriate catalysts. There is good evidence that two or more manganese atoms complexed with protein are involved in this catalysis, taking four electrons from two water molecules (with release of four hydrogen ions). The manganese-protein complex gives up these electrons one at a time via an unidentified carrier Z to P_{680}^+, reducing it to P^{680}. When manganese is selectively removed by chemical treatment, the thylakoids lose the capacity to oxidize water, but all other parts of the electron pathway remain intact.

In light reaction I, P_{700}^+ recovers electrons from plastocyanin (PC), which in turn receives them from intermediate carriers, including the plastoquinone pool and cytochrome b and cytochrome f molecules. The pool of intermediate carriers may receive electrons from water via light reaction II and Q_A and Q_B.

Transfer of electrons from water to ferredoxin via the two light reactions and intermediate carriers is called noncyclic electron flow. Alternately, electrons may be transferred only by light reaction I, in which case they are recycled from ferredoxin back to the intermediate carriers. This process is called cyclic electron flow.

EVIDENCE OF TWO LIGHT REACTIONS

Many lines of evidence support the concept of electron flow via two light reactions. An early study by the U.S. biochemist Robert Emerson employed the algae *Chlorella*, which was illuminated with red light alone, with blue light alone, and with red and blue light at the same time. Oxygen evolution was measured in each case. It was substantial with blue light alone but not with red light alone. With both red and blue light together, the amount of oxygen evolved far exceeded the sum of that seen with blue and red light alone. These experimental data pointed to the existence of two types of light reactions that, when operating in tandem, would yield the highest rate of oxygen evolution. It is now known that light reaction I can use light of a slightly longer wavelength than red (λ = 680 nanometres), while light reaction II requires light with a wavelength of 680 nanometres or shorter.

Since those early studies, the two light reactions have been separated in many ways, including separation of the membrane particles in which each reaction occurs. As discussed previously, lamellae can be disrupted mechanically into fragments that absorb light energy and break the bonds of water molecules (i.e., oxidize water) to produce oxygen, hydrogen ions, and electrons. These electrons can be transferred to ferredoxin, the final electron acceptor of the light stage. No transfer of electrons from water to ferredoxin occurs if the herbicide DCMU is present. The subsequent addition of certain reduced dyes (i.e., electron donors) restores the light reduction of $NADP^+$ but without oxygen production, suggesting that light reaction I but not light reaction II is functioning. It is now known that DCMU blocks the transfer of electrons from Q_A to the PQ pool.

When treated with certain detergents, lamellae can be broken down into smaller particles capable of carrying out single light reactions. One type of particle can absorb light energy, oxidize water, and produce oxygen (light reaction II), but a special dye molecule must be supplied to accept the electrons. In the presence of electron donors, such as a reduced dye, a second type of lamellar particle can absorb light and transfer electrons from the electron donor to ferredoxin (light reaction I).

PHOTOSYSTEMS I AND II

The structural and photochemical properties of the minimum particles capable of performing light reactions I and II have received much study. Treatment of lamellar fragments with neutral detergents releases these particles, designated photosystem I and photosystem II, respectively. Subsequent harsher treatment (with charged detergents) and separation of the individual polypeptides with electrophoretic techniques has helped identify the components of the photosystems. Each photosystem consists of a light harvesting complex and a core complex. Each core complex contains a reaction centre with the pigment (either P_{700} or P_{680}) that can be photochemically oxidized, together with electron acceptors and electron donors. In addition, the core complex has some 40 to 60 chlorophyll molecules bound to proteins. In addition to the light absorbed by the chlorophyll molecules in the core complex, the reaction centres receive a major part of their excitation from the pigments of the light-harvesting complex.

QUANTUM REQUIREMENTS

The quantum requirements of the individual light reactions of photosynthesis are defined as the number of light photons absorbed for the transfer of one electron. The quantum requirement for each light reaction has been found to be approximately one photon. The total number of quanta required, therefore, to transfer the four electrons that result in the formation of one molecule of oxygen via the two light reactions should be four times two, or eight. It appears, however, that additional light is absorbed and used to form ATP by a cyclic photophosphorylation pathway. The actual quantum requirement, therefore, probably is nine to 10.

THE CONVERSION OF LIGHT ENERGY TO ATP

The electron transfers of the light reactions provide the energy for the synthesis of two compounds vital

Chemiosmosis in chloroplasts

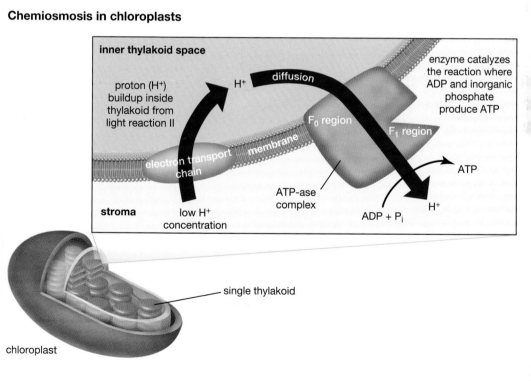

Chemiosmosis in chloroplasts results in the donation of a proton for the production of adenosine triphosphate (ATP) in plants.

to the dark reactions: NADPH and ATP. The previous section explained how noncyclic electron flow results in the reduction of $NADP^+$ to NADPH. In this section, the synthesis of the energy-rich compound ATP is described.

ATP is formed by the addition of a phosphate group to a molecule of adenosine diphosphate (ADP); or to state it in chemical terms, by the phosphorylation of ADP. This reaction requires a substantial input of energy, much of which is captured in the bond that links the added phosphate group to ADP. Because light energy powers this reaction in the chloroplasts, the production of ATP during photosynthesis is referred to as photophosphorylation.

Unlike the production of NADPH, the photophosphorylation of ADP occurs in conjunction with both cyclic and noncyclic electron flow. In fact researchers speculate that the sole purpose of cyclic electron flow may be for photophosphorylation, since this process involves no net transfer of electrons to reducing agents. The relative amounts of cyclic and noncyclic flow may be adjusted in accordance with changing physiological needs for ATP and reduced ferrodoxin and NADPH in chloroplasts. In contrast to electron transfer in light reactions I and II, which can occur in membrane fragments, intact thylakoids are required for efficient photophosphorylation. This requirement stems from the special nature of the mechanism linking photophosphorylation to electron flow in the lamellae.

The theory relating the formation of ATP to electron flow in the membranes of both chloroplasts and mitochondria (the organelles responsible for ATP formation during cellular respiration) was first proposed by the English biochemist Peter Mitchell. This chemiosmotic theory has been somewhat modified to fit later experimental facts, and there is still debate over many of the details. The general features, however, are widely accepted. A central feature is the formation of a hydrogen ion (proton) concentration gradient and an electrical charge across intact lamellae. The potential energy stored by the proton gradient and electrical charge is then used to drive the energetically unfavourable conversion of ADP and inorganic phosphate (P_i) to ATP and water.

The manganese-protein complex associated with light reaction II is exposed to the interior of the thylakoid. Consequently, the oxidation of water during light reaction II leads to release of hydrogen ions (protons) into the inner thylakoid space. Furthermore, it is likely that photoreaction II entails the transfer of electrons across the lamella toward its outer face, so that when plastoquinone molecules are reduced they can receive protons from the outside of the thylakoid. When these reduced plastoquinone molecules are oxidized, giving up electrons to the cytochrome-ironsulfur complex, protons are released inside the thylakoid. Because the lamella is impermeable to them, the release of protons inside the thylakoid by oxidation of both water and plas-toquinone leads to a higher concentration of protons inside the thylakoid than outside it. In other words, a proton gradient is established across the lamella. The movement of electrons (negatively charged particles) outward across the lamella during both light reactions results in the establishment of an electrical charge across the lamella.

An enzyme complex located partly in and on the lamellae catalyzes the reaction in which ATP is formed from ADP and inorganic phosphate. The reverse of this reaction is catalyzed by an enzyme called ATP-ase, hence the enzyme complex is sometimes called an ATP-ase complex. It is also called the coupling factor.

It consists of hydrophilic polypeptides (F_1), which project from the outer surface of the lamellae, and hydrophobic polypeptides (F_0), which are embedded inside the lamellae. Researchers hypothesize that F_0 forms a channel that permits protons to flow through the lamellar membrane to F_1. The enzymes in F_1 then catalyze ATP formation, using both the proton supply and the lamellar transmembrane charge. In summary, the use of light energy for ATP formation occurs indirectly: a proton gradient and electrical charge—built up in or across the lamellae as a consequence of electron flow in the light reactions—provide the energy to drive the synthesis of ATP from ADP and P_i.

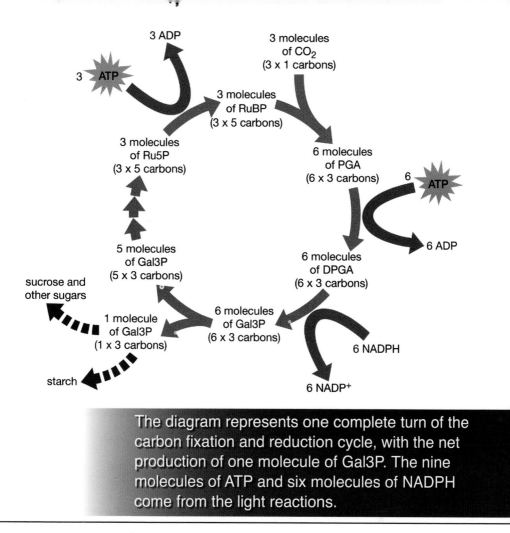

3 ADP

3 ATP

3 molecules of CO$_2$ (3 x 1 carbons)

3 molecules of RuBP (3 x 5 carbons)

3 molecules of Ru5P (3 x 5 carbons)

6 molecules of PGA (6 x 3 carbons)

6 ATP

6 ADP

5 molecules of Gal3P (5 x 3 carbons)

6 molecules of DPGA (6 x 3 carbons)

sucrose and other sugars

1 molecule of Gal3P (1 x 3 carbons)

6 molecules of Gal3P (6 x 3 carbons)

6 NADPH

starch

6 NADP$^+$

The diagram represents one complete turn of the carbon fixation and reduction cycle, with the net production of one molecule of Gal3P. The nine molecules of ATP and six molecules of NADPH come from the light reactions.

CARBON FIXATION AND REDUCTION

The assimilation of carbon into organic compounds is the result of a complex series of enzymatically regulated chemical reactions—the dark reactions. This term is something of a misnomer, for these reactions can take place in either light or darkness. Furthermore, some of the enzymes involved in the so-called dark reactions become inactive in prolonged darkness.

275

EXPLANATION OF THE CARBON PATHWAY

Radioactive isotopes of carbon (^{14}C) and phosphorus (^{32}P) have been valuable in identifying the intermediate compounds formed during carbon assimilation. A photosynthesizing plant does not strongly discriminate between the natural carbon isotopes and ^{14}C. During photosynthesis in the presence of $^{14}CO_2$, the compounds formed become labelled with the radioisotope. During very short exposures, only the first intermediates in the carbon-fixing pathway become labelled. Early investigations showed that some radioactive products were formed even when the light was turned off and the $^{14}CO_2$ was added just afterward in the dark, confirming the nature of the carbon fixation as a "dark" reaction.

The American biochemist Melvin Calvin, a Nobel Prize recipient for his work on the carbon reduction cycle, allowed green plants to photosynthesize in the presence of radioactive carbon dioxide for a few seconds under various experimental conditions. Products that became labelled with radioactive carbon during Calvin's experiments included a three-carbon compound called 3-phosphoglycerate (abbreviated PGA), sugar phosphates, amino acids, sucrose, and carboxylic acids. When photosynthesis was stopped after two seconds, the principal radioactive product was PGA, which therefore was identified as the first compound formed during carbon dioxide fixation in green plants.

DISCOVERING THE CARBON PATHWAYS OF PHOTOSYNTHESIS

American biochemist Melvin Calvin (1911–1997) began his Nobel prize-winning work on photosynthesis at the University of California, Berkeley, in 1946. After adding carbon dioxide with trace amounts of radioactive carbon-14 to an illuminated suspension of the single-cell green alga *Chlorella pyrenoidosa*, he stopped the alga's growth at different stages and used paper chromatography to isolate and identify the minute quantities of radioactive compounds. This enabled him to identify most of the chemical reactions in the intermediate steps of photosynthesis—the process in which carbon dioxide is converted into carbohydrates. He discovered the "Calvin cycle," in which the "dark" photosynthetic reactions are impelled by compounds produced in the "light" reactions that occur on absorption of light by chlorophyll to yield oxygen. Also using isotopic tracer techniques, he followed the path of oxygen in photosynthesis. This was the first use of a carbon-14 tracer to explain a chemical pathway. He was awarded the Nobel Prize for Chemistry in 1961 for his work in discovering these chemical pathways of photosynthesis.

Calvin's research also included work on electronic, photoelectronic, and photochemical behaviour of porphyrins; chemical evolution and organic geochemistry, including organic constituents of lunar rocks for the U.S. National Aeronautics and Space Administration (NASA); free radical reactions; the effect of deuterium

(continued on the next page)

(continued from the previous page)

("heavy hydrogen") on biochemical reactions; chemical and viral carcinogenesis; artificial photosynthesis ("synthetic chloroplasts"); radiation chemistry; the biochemistry of learning; brain chemistry; philosophy of science; and processes leading to the origin of life.

Calvin's bioorganic group eventually required more space, so he designed the new Laboratory of Chemical Biodynamics (the "Roundhouse" or "Calvin Carousel"). This circular building contained open laboratories and numerous windows but few walls to encourage the interdisciplinary interaction that he had carried out with his photosynthesis group at the old Radiation Laboratory. He directed this laboratory until his mandatory age retirement in 1980, when it was renamed the Melvin Calvin Laboratory. Although officially retired, he continued to come to his office until 1996 to work with a small research group.

Further studies with ^{14}C as well as with inorganic phosphate labelled with ^{32}P led to the mapping of the carbon fixation and reduction pathway called the reductive pentose phosphate cycle (RPP cycle). An additional pathway for carbon transport in certain plants was later discovered in other laboratories. All the steps in these pathways can be carried out in the laboratory by isolated enzymes in the dark. Several steps require the ATP or NADPH generated by the light reactions. In addition, some of the enzymes are fully active only when conditions simulate those in green cells exposed to light. In vivo, these enzymes are active during photosynthesis but not in the dark.

THE REDUCTIVE PENTOSE PHOSPHATE CYCLE

The RPP cycle, in which carbon is fixed, reduced, and utilized, involves the formation of intermediate sugar phosphates in a cyclic sequence. One complete RPP cycle incorporates three molecules of carbon dioxide and produces one molecule of the three-carbon compound glyceraldehyde-3-phosphate (Gal_3P). This sugar phosphate usually is either exported from the chloroplasts or is converted to starch.

ATP and NADPH formed during the light reactions are utilized for key steps in this pathway and provide the energy and reducing equivalents (i.e., electrons) to drive the sequence. For each molecule of carbon dioxide that is fixed, two molecules of NADPH and three molecules of ATP from the light reactions are required. The overall reaction can be represented as follows:

The cycle is composed of four stages: (1) carboxylation, (2) reduction, (3) isomerization/condensation/dismutation, and (4) phosphorylation.

CARBOXYLATION AND REDUCTION

The initial incorporation of carbon dioxide, which is catalyzed by the enzyme ribulose 1,5-bisphosphate carboxylase, proceeds by the addition of carbon dioxide to the five carbon compound ribulose 1,5-bisphosphate (RuBP) and the splitting of the resulting unstable six-carbon compound into two molecules of PGA, a three-carbon compound. This reaction occurs three times during each complete turn of the cycle. Thus, six molecules of PGA are produced. The six molecules of PGA are first phosphorylated with ATP by the enzyme PGA-kinase, yielding six molecules of 1,3-diphosphoglycerate (DPGA). These then are reduced with NADPH and the enzyme glyceraldehyde-3-phosphate dehydrogenase to give six molecules of Gal3P. These reactions are the reverse of two steps of the process glycolysis in cellular respiration.

SUBSEQUENT REACTIONS

For each complete RPP cycle, one of the Gal3P molecules, with its three carbon atoms, is the net product and may be transferred out of the chloroplast or converted to starch inside the chloroplast. For the cycle to regenerate, the other five Gal3P molecules (with a total of 15 carbon atoms) must be converted back to three molecules of five-carbon RuBP. The conversion of Gal3P to RuBP begins with a complex series of enzymatically regulated reactions that lead to the synthesis of the five-carbon compound ribulose-5-phosphate (Ru5P). The occurrence of this complex series entails isomerization, condensation, and dismutation reactions. The three molecules of Ru5P are converted to the carboxylation substrate, RuBP, by the enzyme phosphoribulokinase, using ATP. This reaction, shown below, completes the cycle.

REGULATION OF THE CYCLE

Photosynthesis cannot occur at night, but the respiratory process of glycolysis—which uses some of the same reactions as the RPP cycle, except in the reverse—does take place. Thus, some steps in the RPP cycle would be wasteful if allowed to occur in the dark because they would counteract the reactions of glycolysis. For this reason, some enzymes of the RPP cycle are "turned off" (i.e., become inactive) in the dark.

Even in the presence of light, changes in physiological conditions frequently necessitate adjustments in the relative rates of reactions of the RPP cycle, so that enzymes for some reactions change in their catalytic activity. These alterations in enzyme activity typically are brought about by changes in levels of such chloroplast components as reduced ferredoxin, acids, and soluble components (e.g., P_i and magnesium ions).

PRODUCTS OF CARBON REDUCTION

The most important use of Gal3P is its export from the chloroplasts to the cytoplasm of green cells, where it is used for biosynthesis of products needed by the plant. In land plants, a principal product is sucrose, which is translocated from the green cells of the leaves to other parts of the plant. Other key products include the carbon skeletons of certain primary amino acids, such as alanine, glutamate, and aspartate. To complete the synthesis of these compounds, amino groups are added to the appropriate carbon skeletons made from Gal3P. Sulfur amino acids such as cysteine are formed by adding sulfhydryl groups and amino groups. Other biosynthesis pathways lead from Gal3P to lipids, pigments, and most of the constituents of green cells.

Starch synthesis and accumulation in the chloroplasts occurs particularly when photosynthetic carbon fixation exceeds the needs of the plant. Under such circumstances, sugar phosphates accumulate in the cytoplasm, binding cytoplasmic P_i. The export of Gal3P from the chloroplasts is tied to a one-for-one exchange of P_i for Gal3P, so less cytoplasmic P_i results in decreased export of Gal3P and decreased P_i in the chloroplast. These changes trigger alterations in the activities of regulated enzymes, leading in turn to increased starch synthesis. This starch can be broken down at night and used as a source of reduced carbon and energy for the physiological needs of the plant. Too much starch in the chloroplasts leads to diminished rates of photosynthesis, however. Thus, under what would seem to be the ideal photosynthetic conditions of a bright, warm day, many plants in fact have slower rates of photosynthesis in the afternoon.

PHOTORESPIRATION

Under conditions of high light intensity, hot weather, and water limitation, the productivity of the RPP cycle is limited in many plants by the occurrence of photorespiration. This process converts sugar phosphates back to carbon dioxide; it is initiated by the oxygenation of RuBP (i.e., the combination of gaseous oxygen $[O_2]$ with RuBP). This oxygenation reaction yields only one molecule of PGA and one molecule of a two-carbon acid, phosphoglycollate, which is subsequently converted in part to carbon dioxide. The reaction of oxygen with RuBP is in direct competition with the carboxylation reaction (CO_2 + RuBP) that initiates the RPP cycle and is, in fact, catalyzed by the same protein, ribulose 1,5-bisphosphate carboxylase. The relative concentrations of oxygen and carbon dioxide within the chloroplasts determine whether oxygenation or carboxylation is favoured. The concentration of oxygen inside the chloroplasts may be higher than atmospheric (20 percent) owing to photosynthetic oxygen evolution, whereas the internal carbon dioxide concentration may be lower than atmospheric (0.035 percent) owing to photosynthetic uptake. Any increase in the internal carbon dioxide pressure tends to help the carboxylation reaction compete more effectively with oxygenation.

CARBON FIXATION VIA C$_4$ ACIDS

Certain plants—including the important crops sugarcane and corn (maize), as well as other diverse species believed to have evolved in the drier tropical areas—have developed a special mechanism of carbon fixation that largely prevents photorespiration. The leaves of these plants have special anatomy and biochemistry. In particular, photosynthetic functions are divided between mesophyll and bundle sheath leaf cells. The carbon fixation pathway begins in the mesophyll cells, where carbon dioxide is added to the three-carbon acid phosphoenolpyruvate (PEPA) by an enzyme called phosphoenolpyruvate carboxylase. The product of this reaction is the four-carbon acid oxaloacetate, which is reduced to malate, another four-carbon acid, in one form of C$_4$ pathway. Malate then is translocated to bundle sheath cells, which are located near the vascular system of the leaf. There, malate enters the chloroplasts and is oxidized and decarboxylated (i.e., loses CO_2) by malic enzyme. This yields carbon dioxide, which is fed into the RPP cycle of the bundle sheath cells, and pyruvate, a three-carbon acid that is translocated back to the mesophyll cells. In the mesophyll chloroplasts, the enzyme pyruvate orthophosphate dikinase (PPDK) uses ATP and P$_i$ to convert pyruvate back to PEPA, completing the C$_4$ cycle. There are several variations of this pathway in different species. For example, the amino acids aspartate and alanine can substitute for malate and pyruvate in some species.

The C_4 pathway acts as a shuttle for carrying carbon dioxide into the chloroplasts of the bundle sheath cells, where it is used in carbohydrate synthesis. The resulting higher level of internal carbon dioxide in these chloroplasts serves to increase the ratio of carboxylation to oxygenation, thus minimizing photorespiration. Although the plant must expend extra energy to drive this shuttle, the energy loss is more than compensated by the near elimination of photorespiration under conditions where it would otherwise occur. Sugarcane and certain other plants that employ this pathway have the highest annual yields of biomass of all species.

THE MOLECULAR BIOLOGY OF PHOTOSYNTHESIS

Oxygenic photosynthesis occurs in both prokaryotic cells (cyanophytes) and eukaryotic cells (algae and higher plants). In eukaryotic cells, which contain chloroplasts and a nucleus, the genetic information needed for the reproduction of the photosynthetic apparatus is contained partly in the chloroplast chromosome and partly in chromosomes of the nucleus. For example, the carboxylation enzyme ribulose 1,5-bisphosphate carboxylase is a large protein molecule comprising a complex of eight large polypeptide subunits and eight small polypeptide subunits. The gene for the large subunits is located in the chloroplast chromosome, while the gene for the small subunits is in the nucleus. Transcription of the DNA of the nuclear gene yields messenger RNA (mRNA) that encodes the information for the synthesis of the small polypeptides. During this synthesis, which occurs on the cytoplasmic ribosomes, some extra amino acid residues are added to form a recognition leader on the end of the polypeptide chain. This leader is recognized by special receptor sites on the outer chloroplast membrane. These receptor sites then allow the polypeptide to penetrate the membrane and enter the chloroplast. The leader is removed and the small subunits combine with the large subunits, which have been synthesized on chloroplast ribosomes according to mRNA transcribed from the chloroplast DNA. The expression of nuclear genes that code for proteins needed in the chloroplasts appears to be under control of events in the chloroplasts in some cases. For example, the synthesis of some nuclear-encoded chloroplast enzymes may occur only when light is absorbed by chloroplasts.

CHAPTER

7

BIOLUMINESCENCE

B iological systems utilize and are affected by light in several different ways. For example, whereas certain organisms can harness light for energy production in the process of photosynthesis, these same organisms are also susceptible to injury from intense light exposure or may be rendered more sensitive to light through various photodynamic reactions. In other instances, organisms may emit light through a process known as bioluminescence. Bioluminescence occurs in a wide range of organisms and results from a chemical reaction that produces radiant energy very efficiently, giving off very little heat.

Bioluminescence is the emission of light by an organism or by a test-tube biochemical system derived from an organism. It could be the ghostly glow of bacteria on decaying meat or fish, the shimmering phosphorescence of protozoans in tropical seas, or the flickering signals of fireflies. The phenomenon occurs sporadically in a wide range of protists and animals, from bacteria and fungi to insects, marine invertebrates, and fish. But it is not known to exist naturally in true plants or in amphibians, reptiles, birds, or mammals. Bioluminescence results from chemiluminescence, a chemical reaction in which the conversion of chemical energy to radiant energy is direct and virtually 100 percent efficient. In other words, very little heat is given off in the process. For this reason the emission is called cold light, or luminescence.

BIOLOGICAL FUNCTION OF BIOLUMINESCENCE

Light production appears to be associated with the protection and survival of a species. This is quite clear in certain squids, who secrete a luminous cloud to confuse an enemy and make an escape, and in many deep-sea fishes who dangle luminous lures to attract prey or who show light organs to disguise their form from enemies, frighten predators, or simply light the way in the darkness of the ocean deeps. The survival value of bioluminescence is indisputable for many organisms who use their flashes as species-recognition and mating signals. In *Photinus pyralis*, a common North American firefly, the male flashes spontaneously while in flight, emitting on the average a 0.3-second flash every 5.5 seconds if the temperature is 25°C (77°F). The females watch from the ground and wait for a male to flash. Upon seeing a flash, a female flashes a response after an interval of about two seconds. It is this response that attracts the male. The female is unable to identify a male by his flashing. Thus it is the male that recognizes the correct signal—i.e., interval between flashes—and seeks out the female. The interval between the male's signal and the female's response, therefore,

Only female anglerfish have the "fishing rod" and luminous "bait" protruding from the head that are used to attract prey.

is crucial. Similar specific recognition codes are used by many species of fireflies. Other fireflies possibly rely on colour differences in the light signals between sexes.

The functional role of bioluminescence in lower organisms such as bacteria, dinoflagellates, and fungi is difficult to discern. Partly because the glow of luminous bacteria is extinguished when oxygen is removed, it has been suggested that the bioluminescent reaction was originally used to remove oxygen toxic to primitive types of bacteria that developed during a time when oxygen was absent or very rare in Earth's atmosphere. The metabolic reaction that combines the oxygen with a reducing substance (luciferin) liberates sufficient energy to excite a molecule in the organism to emit visible radiation. Most of those luminous primitive organisms have subsequently developed systems of utilizing oxygen, but they have retained the luminescent capability as parts of related metabolic pathways or for some survival value that luminescence may confer on the organism.

TYPES OF BIOLUMINESCENT ORGANISMS

Luminous species are widely scattered taxonomically, with no clear-cut pattern discernible. Many luminous shrimps are known but no luminous

Bitter oyster (*Panellus stipticus*) is a saprophytic fungus capable of bioluminescence. Classified in the family Mycenaceae, the species is found in Eurasia, Australia, and North America.

crab. Many luminous squids are known but only a single luminous octopus (*Callistoctopus arakawai* of Japan). Again, luminous centipedes and millipedes are not uncommon, but luminous scorpions and spiders are apparently nonexistent. Many plantlike protists exhibit bioluminescence, but no luminous true plant is known.

Almost half the animal phyla contain luminous forms, but the number of representatives is very small compared with the total number of known animal species. The protists are not so rich in luminous species but are greatest in sheer abundance, especially in tropical seas. In fact, the majority of luminous organisms are marine.

The ocean surface in many parts of the tropics is dense with single-celled luminous planktonic organisms, primarily dinoflagellates, that glow when stimulated mechanically, as by the churning of the waves, or, when washed ashore, by the pressure of a foot. Some organisms exhibit a 24-hour rhythm of light intensity, highest at night and lowest during the day.

Among crustaceans, luminous species are especially remarkable in the copepods, shrimps, and ostracods. Luminous copepods are widely distributed throughout the world's waters. Some are surface dwellers, while others live in the deep sea. Two famous groups of luminous copepods are *Pleuromma* and *Metridia*. Some shrimps (*Hoplophorus*) emit a luminous secretion from luminous organs, while others possess true light organs (*photophores*), which consist of a lens, reflector, and light-emitting photogenic cells. Of the three or four species of the ostracod genus *Cypridina* known to be luminous, the most famous is *Cypridina hilgendorfii*, found in the coastal waters and sands of Japan. This tiny, shelled organism, which ejects a blue luminous secretion into the water when disturbed, may be collected and dried for the light-emitting components, which are active indefinitely.

Other organisms responsible for large patches of light in the ocean are jellyfish and other coelenterates and comb jellies (ctenophores). A large proportion of the floating, transparent siphonophores and the feathery, bottom-dwelling sea pens are luminous. Many of the hydroids and jellyfish are also luminous. Sea pens (*Pennatula*), sea cactus (*Cavernularia*), and sea pansy (*Renilla*) are colonies, which upon stimulation generate a wave of luminous light that travels down the organism. The luminescence in these organisms appears to be under nervous control.

Among annelids, marine worms and earthworms both contain luminous forms. *Odontosyllis*, the fire worm of Bermuda, swarms in great numbers a few days after the full moon. Female worms, about 2 cm (almost 1 inch) in length, rise to the surface shortly after sunset and swim in circles while ejecting a luminous secretion. Smaller male worms swim to where the females are circling and mate. The male is also luminous, but the light is intermittent and of intracellular character. It is not certain whether luminescence has any relationship to mating, since nonluminous *Odontosyllis* exhibits similar courtship behaviour. *Chaetopterus* spends its life in a tube of parchment membrane, with openings at both ends. It luminesces when disturbed, but it is doubtful whether the luminescence has any special purpose. *Polynoe* and *Polycirrus* are luminous annelids that usually live in sand or rock. Luminous mollusks include *Pholas* (a bivalve), *Phyllirrhoe* (a floating nudibranch),

Planaxis (a marine gastropod), Latia (a freshwater limpet), and squids (cephalopods).

The luminous squids and deep-sea fishes possess the most complicated light organs. They consist of photogenic cells, reflector, lens body, and, in certain cases, colour filters. Of the open-ocean squids (oegopsids) such as *Lycoteuthis, Histioteuthis,* and *Enoploteuthis,* as many as 75 percent are self-luminous (i.e., light results not from symbiotic luminous bacteria but from an internal biochemical reaction).

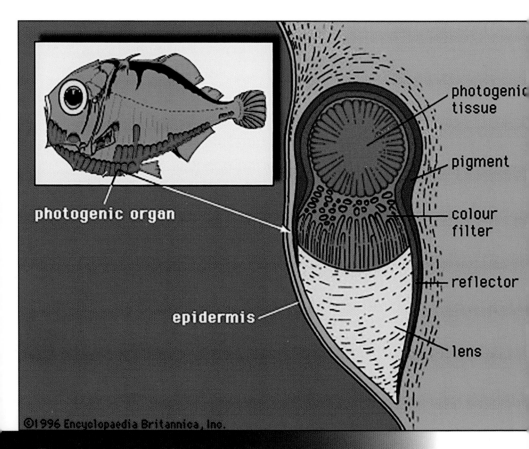

photogenic tissue

pigment

colour filter

reflector

lens

photogenic organ

epidermis

©1996 Encyclopaedia Britannica, Inc.

Tranverse section of a photogenic organ of a hatchetfish (*Polyipnus spinosus*)

In deep-sea squids, the light organ is often found on the eyelid or on the eyeball itself. In others—such as *Watasenia scintillans*—light organs are present also at the end of the tentacles and over other surfaces of the body.

Deep-sea anglerfish, hatchetfish, and lantern fish are among the best-known luminescent fishes. In most such fishes, luminescence is produced intracellularly, with the light being emitted by special cells called photocytes. The anatomical structure of the luminous organs of many fishes is similar to that of squids. Deep-sea fishes have photophores along the body, under the eyes, and often on barbels or antennae. The typical luminous organ consists of a lens, luminous body, colour filter, and reflector. The light is often under the fish's nervous control, and after death the ability to luminesce disappears rapidly. Whether the light-producing components are developed by the fish or ingested by the fish is not clear. A distinct possibility exists that a fish feeds on crustaceans such as *Cypridina* organisms and utilizes their light-emitting components for its own light production.

The light organs, or photophores, of many deep-sea fishes are placed on the ventral and lateral surfaces of the body, and the light is emitted downward and outward. Such an arrangement is believed to allow the light of the photophores to be used to match the intensity of sunlight penetrating from above, thus concealing the fish's own shadow from a predator below. Some lantern fishes possess, in addition, a large nasal organ. Others have a patch of luminous tissue in the tail region. In deep-sea anglerfishes, the first dorsal spine is turned forward into an elongated rod, from the end of which dangles a luminous organ. When an unsuspecting prey approaches the luminous lure, it is engulfed in the fish's large jaw.

A few genera of deep-sea fishes and several families of shallow-water fishes produce light by virtue of harbouring symbiotic luminous bacteria within light organs. This type of organ is endowed with a rich blood supply that nourishes and maintains the luminous bacteria. It appears that each fish species becomes infected with a specific bacterial type. The bacteria-filled organ is continuously luminous, but the light can be controlled either by melanophores scattered over the surface of the organ or by a black membrane that may be mechanically drawn over the organ. Control is brought about by the contraction and expansion of melanophores, or pigment granules. Expansion of the melanophores cuts off the light, whereas contraction allows light to pass through. The well-known flashlight fishes (*Photoblepharon*) of Indonesia possess large light organs beneath the eyes. The light is extinguished when a fold of black skin is drawn upward over the organ.

An indirect-emission type of luminous organ is present in some fish. The luminous organ is connected to the gut via a short duct and is often embedded in tissue. The light passes to the outside through the translucent keel and ventral muscles, as in *Leiognathus*, *Acropoma* (lanternbellies), and *Archamia*.

Among other higher animals, the chordate subphylum *Tunicata* contains luminous forms. The genus *Pyrosoma* includes several species that account for the brilliant luminescence among macroplanktons of the seas, giving rise to the name "fire body." *Pyrosoma* is a floating colonial form, pelagic and translucent. The colonies usually reach a length of 3 to 10 cm (about 1 to 4 inches), and each individual is about 5 mm (0.2 inch) long.

Luminous microorganisms and plantlike protists are represented by only two groups, bacteria and fungi. Luminous bacteria are all marine forms, requiring salt for growth and luminescence, and are widely distributed throughout the oceans of the world. The most common are *Vibrio* and *Photobacterium* species. While luminous bacteria come in various shapes, they do not form clusters or chains, as do many other bacteria. The light of an individual bacterium, of course, cannot be seen with the naked eye, but the light from a liquid or agar culture containing billions of bacteria is readily visible. The light is bluish and continuous. Many luminous bacteria live in the light organs of fish and squids, without adversely affecting their hosts. Small, whitish, luminous fungi ("foxfire") commonly grow on dead wood of forests, particularly where the ground is moist and wet. These forms predominate in the tropics. The lightoffungi ranges from blue to green and yellow, depending on the species. Among the large luminous forms are *Pleurotus lampas* of Australia and the jack-o'lantern (*Clitocybe illudens*) of the United States, which reach approximately 13 cm (about 5 inches) in diameter.

Luminosity among land animals is not associated with any particular habitat, but almost all these forms are nocturnal. The centipede *Orphaneus*, widely distributed in tropical Asia, gives off luminous secretions from each segment. The entire body of *Luminodesmus sequoiae*, a millipede found in the Sierra Nevada (mountains) of California, glows with a diffuse light. Luminous insects include some true flies (order Diptera), notably *Arachnocampa luminosa*, the larva of which luminesces a greenish blue from a knob at the end of its body. The larvae dangle at the ends of filaments that hang from the ceilings of caves in New Zealand. Luminous beetles include the fireflies and the elaterid *Pyrophorus* (the click beetle, or cucujo in South America). The luminescent larvae of fireflies and some luminescent wingless adults are known as glowworms. The female *Diplocladon hasseltii*, called starworm, or diamond worm, gives off a continuous greenish blue luminescence from three spots on each segment of the body, forming three longitudinal rows of light, the appearance of which inspired the common name night train. *Phrixothrix*, the railroad worm, possesses two longitudinal rows, with a red luminous spot on the head.

The limpet *Latia neritoides*, found in streams around Auckland, N.Z., is the only strictly freshwater luminous form known. The so-called firefly shrimp (*hotaru ebi*) is found in Lake Suwa, Japan, but the light is from luminous bacteria that infect the shrimp and kill it in about 24 hours.

BIOCHEMICAL EVENTS OF LIGHT EMISSION

In most bioluminescent organisms, the essential light-emitting components are the oxidizable organic molecule luciferin and the enzyme luciferase, which are specific for different organisms. The present custom is to use generic names according to origin—e.g., firefly luciferin and luciferase, *Cypridina* luciferin and luciferase. The luciferin-luciferase reaction is actually an enzymesubstrate reaction in which luciferin, the substrate, is oxidized by molecular oxygen, the reaction being catalyzed by the enzyme luciferase, with the consequent emission of light. The light emission continues until all the luciferin is oxidized. This type of reaction is found

BIOLUMINESCENCE IN MEDICAL AND BIOLOGICAL RESEARCH

The reactions of bioluminescent and fluorescent molecules can have useful applications in scientific research. For example, the luminescent reaction of the firefly has been used as an assay method for the determination of ATP. The glow of a specially blended extract of firefly lanterns eventually dims and disappears as ATP is broken down. The addition of fresh ATP, either as a pure chemical or as a constituent of a tissue extract, immediately restores the luminescence. The intensity of the glow is a direct measure of the amount of ATP present in the extract. This assay method has been widely used in medical and biological research to determine the amount of ATP present in extracts of cells and tissues. The study of reactions involving ATP has led to a detailed understanding of the mechanisms of energy conversion in cells. The firefly reaction is one of the few reactions in which ATP is directly involved with light emission. All other bioluminescent reactions involve compounds that are chemically distinct from ATP.

Another promising discovery was that of the green fluorescent protein (GFP), a naturally occurring substance in the jellyfish *Aequorea victoria* that is used as a tool to make visible the actions of certain cells. Osamu Shimomura (1928–), Martin Chalfie (1947–), and Roger Y. Tsein (1952–2016) received the 2008 Nobel Prize in Chemistry for their work with GFP.

The *Aequorea victoria* jellyfish is visible in a dark aquarium thanks to the green fluorescent protein.

Shimomura first identified the GFP in the 1960s. The visual signal that GFP provides allows scientists to probe protein activity, such as when and where proteins are produced and how different proteins or parts of proteins move and approach each other within a cell. Subsequent discoveries by his corecipients opened a vast set of opportunities for the utilization of GFP in studying biological processes at the molecular level.

American biochemist Douglas Prasher analyzed the chromophore in GFP in the 1980s and subsequently

(continued on the next page)

(continued from the previous page)

found and cloned the gene responsible for making GFP. In 1993 Chalfie showed that the gene that instructs the cell to make GFP could be embedded in the nucleic acids of other organisms, first in the bacterium *E. coli* and then in the transparent nematode *Caenorhabditis elegans*, so that they would make their own GFP. This discovery opened the possibility of using GFP in virtually any organism. Tsien then showed, beginning in 1994, that oxygen is required for GFP fluorescence and that point mutations in the gene could shift the wavelength and intensity of the fluorescence—in other words, he discovered how to make the proteins glow more brightly and in different colours. That find made it possible to study different processes in the same cell simultaneously. Tsien also helped to determine the structure of GFP and described how to use GFP and its variants to study the role and behaviour of calcium ions in living systems.

in fireflies, *Cypridina, Latia,* and many types of fish, such as lantern fish, hatchetfish, *Apogon,* and *Parapriaeanthus.*

In firefly luminescence, the substance ATP initially reacts with firefly luciferase, magnesium ion, and firefly luciferin to form a complex (luciferase-luciferyladenylate) and pyrophosphate. This complex then reacts with molecular oxygen to emit light. Enough energy is liberated in the last step to convert the electronic configuration of the luciferase-luciferyl-adenylate complex from a low-energy ground state to a high-energy excited state. The high-energy complex then loses energy by radiating a photon of visible light and returns to the ground state.

Luminescent bacteria employ the enzymatic oxidation of reduced flavin mononucleotide ($FMNH_2$). In the complete reaction, bacterial luciferase reacts with $FMNH_2$ and oxygen to form a long-lived intermediate complex, which then reacts with a long-chain aliphatic aldehyde molecule (e.g., decanal) to emit light.

BIOLOGICAL EFFECTS OF LIGHT

Life could not exist on Earth without light from the Sun. Plants utilize the energy of the Sun's rays in the process of photosynthesis to produce carbohydrates and proteins, which serve as basic organic sources of food and energy for animals. Light has a powerful regulating influence on many biologic systems. Most of the strong ultraviolet rays of the Sun, which are hazardous, are effectively absorbed by the upper atmosphere. At high altitudes and near the Equator, the ultraviolet intensity is greater than at sea level or at northern latitudes.

Ultraviolet light of very short wavelength, below 2200 angstroms, is highly toxic for cells. In the intermediate range, the greatest killing effectiveness on cells is at about 2600 angstroms. The nucleic acids of the cell, of which genetic material is composed, strongly absorb rays in this region. This wavelength, readily available in mercury vapour, xenon, or hydrogen arc lamps, has great effectiveness for germicidal purification of the air.

Since penetration of visible and ultraviolet light in body tissues is small, only the effects of light on skin and on the visual apparatus are of consequence. When incident light exerts its action on the skin without additional external predisposing factors, scientists speak of intrinsic action. In contrast, a number of chemical or biologic agents may condition the skin for action of light. These latter phenomena are grouped under photodynamic action. Visible light, when administered following lethal doses of ultraviolet, is capable of causing recovery of the cells exposed. This phenomenon, referred to as photorecovery, has led to the discovery of various enzyme systems that are capable of restoring damaged nucleic acids in genes to their normal form. It is probable that photorecovery mechanisms are continually operative in some plants exposed to the direct action of sunlight.

The surface of Earth is protected from the lethal ultraviolet rays of the Sun by the top layers of the atmosphere, which absorb far ultraviolet, and by ozone molecules in the stratosphere, which absorb most of the near ultraviolet. Even so, it is believed that an enzymatic mechanism operating in the skin cells of individuals continually repairs the damage caused by ultraviolet rays to the nucleic acids of the genes. Chlorofluorocarbons once used in aerosol spray products and in various technical applications were found to deplete the stratospheric ozone layer, thus exposing persons to more intense ultraviolet radiation at ground level.

There is some evidence to indicate that not only overall light intensity but also special compositions have differential effects on organisms. For example, in pumpkins, red light favours the production of pistillate flowers, and blue light leads to development of staminate flowers. The ratio of females to males in guppies is increased by red light. Red light also appears to accelerate the rate of proliferation of some tumours in special strains of mice. The intensity of incident light has an influence on the development of light-sensing organs. The eyes of primates reared in complete darkness, for instance, are much retarded in development.

The wavelength of light that produces sunburn also can cause inflammation of the cornea of the eye. This is what occurs in snow blindness or after exposure to strong ultraviolet light sources. Unusual sensitivities have been reported. Ultraviolet light, like infrared or penetrating radiations, can also cause cataract of the eye lens, a condition characterized by denatured protein in the fibrous cells forming the lens. The retina usually is not reached by ultraviolet light, but large doses of visible and infrared light can irreversibly bleach the visual pigments, as in sun blindness. Numerous pathological conditions of the eye are accompanied by abnormal light sensitivity and pain, a condition that is known as photophobia. The pain appears to be associated with reflex movements of the iris and reflex dilation of the blood vessels of the conjunctiva. Workers exposed to ultraviolet-light sources or to atomic flashes need to wear protective glasses.

INTRINSIC ACTION

Light is essential to the human body because of its biosynthetic action. Ultraviolet light induces the conversion of ergosterol and other vitamin precursors present in normal skin to vitamin D, an essential factor for normal calcium deposition in growing bones. While some ultraviolet light appears desirable for the formation of vitamin D, an excess amount is deleterious. Humans have a delicate adaptive mechanism that regulates light exposure of the more sensitive deeper layers of the skin. The transmission of light depends on the thickness of the upper layers of the skin and on the degree of skin pigmentation. All persons, with the exception of albinos, are born with varying amounts of melanin pigment in their skin. Exposure to light further enhances the pigmentation already present and can induce production of new pigment granules. The therapeutic possibilities of sunlight and ultraviolet light became apparent around 1900, with popularization of the idea that exposure of the whole body to sunlight promotes health.

By that time, it was already known that large doses of ultraviolet radiation cause sunburn, the wavelength of about 2800 angstroms being most effective. It induces reddening and swelling of the skin (owing to dilation of the blood vessels), usually accompanied by pain. In the course of recovery, epidermal cells are proliferated, melanin is secreted, and the outer corneal layer of dead cells is thickened. In 1928 it was first shown clearly that prolonged or repeated exposure to ultraviolet light leads to the delayed development of skin cancer. The fact that ultraviolet light, like X radiation, is mutagenic may explain its ability to cause skin cancer, but the detailed mechanism of cancer induction is not yet completely understood. There seems very little doubt, however, that skin cancer in humans is in some cases correlated with prolonged exposure to large doses of sunlight. Among blacks who are protected by rich melanin formation and thickened corneal structure of the skin, incidence of cancer of the skin is several times less frequent than it is among whites living at the same latitude.

PHOTODYNAMIC ACTION

There are a number of diseases in humans and other animals in which light sensitivity is involved. For example, hydroa manifests itself in blisters on parts of the body exposed to sunlight. It has been suggested that this disease results from a light-sensitive porphyrin compound found in the blood.

Actually there are many organic substances and various materials of biologic origin that make cells sensitive to light. When eosin is added to a suspension of human red blood corpuscles exposed to light, the red corpuscles will break up in a process called hemolysis. Other typical photodynamic substances are rose bengal, hematoporphyrin, and phylloerythrin—all are dyes capable of fluorescence. Their toxicity manifests itself only in the presence of light and oxygen.

Some diseases in domestic animals result from ingestion of plants having photodynamic pigments. For example, St. Johnswort's disease is caused by the plant *Hypericum*. Fagopyrism results from eating buckwheat.

In geeldikopp ("yellow thick head"), the photodynamic agent is produced in the animal's own intestinal tract from chlorophyll derived from plants.

In humans the heritable condition of porphyria frequently is associated with light sensitivity, as are a number of somewhat ill-defined dermatologic conditions that result from exposure to sunlight. The recessively inherited rare disease xeroderma pigmentosum also is associated with light exposure; it usually results in death at an early age from tumours of the skin that develop on exposed areas. The cells of such individuals possess a serious genetic defect: they lack the ability to repair nucleic-acid lesions caused by ultraviolet light. Certain drugs (e.g., sulfanilamide) sensitize some persons to sunlight. Many cases are known in which ingestion of or skin contact with a photodynamic substance was followed by increased light sensitivity.

DEVELOPMENT AND BIOLOGIC RHYTHMS

In addition to its photosynthetic effect, light exerts an influence on growth and spatial orientation of plants. This phototropism is associated with yellow pigments and is particularly marked in blue light. The presence of illumination is a profound modifier of the cellular activities in plants as well. For example, while some species of blue-green algae carry out photosynthesis in the presence of light, they do not undergo cell division.

Diffuse sensitivity to light also exists in several phyla of animals. Many protozoans react to light.

CHROMATOPHORE

A chromatophore is a pigment-containing cell in the deeper layers of the skin of animals. Depending on the colour of their pigment, chromatophores are called melanophores (black), erythrophores (red), xanthophores (yellow), or leucophores (white). The distribution of the chromatophores and the pigments they contain determine the colour patterns of an organism.

In fishes, chromatophores are found in both epidermis and dermis. Rapid colour change, by which some fishes can adapt to a change of background, is brought about by redistribution of the pigment within the cell boundaries. Slow, long-term changes involve alterations in the numbers of cells or in the amount of pigment they contain. Chromatophores are also present in amphibians and reptiles, but not in birds or mammals, which possess pigment cells called melanocytes. Pigment cells—chromatophores and melanocytes alike—are influenced by melanocyte-stimulating hormones of the pituitary.

Chameleons, frogs, and octopuses change colour under the influence of light. Such changes are ascribed to special organs known as chromatophores, which are under the influence of the nervous system or endocrine system. The breeding habits and migration of some birds are set in motion by small consecutive changes in the daily cycle of light.

Light is an important controlling agent of recurrent daily physiological alterations (circadian rhythms) in many animals, including humans in all likelihood. Lighting cycles have been shown to be important in regulating several types of endocrine function: the daily variation in light intensity keeps the secretion of adrenal steroids in synchrony. The annual breeding cycles in many mammals and birds appear to be regulated by light. Ambient light somehow influences the secretions of a tiny gland, the pineal body, located near the cerebellum. The pineal body, under the action of enzymes, produces melanotonin, which in higher concentrations slows down the estrous cycle. Low levels of melanotonin, caused by exposure of animals to light, accelerates estrus. Light stimulates the retina, and information is then transmitted by sympathetic nerves to the pineal body.

CONCLUSION

Scientists continue to make fascinating technological advances and discoveries about the biochemical reactions that make life possible. For example, despite many years of research, biochemists are still discovering and characterizing the enzymes that drive metabolism. They can also now use computer technologies to re-create precise chemical structures and reactions and predict their outcomes. Biochemical studies have had a significant impact on furthering the understanding of metabolic activities in human cells, particularly in stem cells (undifferentiated cells) and in cells affected by disease. Research in these areas could help scientists develop therapies for degenerative diseases (such as Parkinson disease and Alzheimer disease) or genetic conditions. Closer examination of biochemical reactions in plants, bacteria, and bioluminescent species may help explain how life first evolved on Earth and lead to other breakthroughs in the fields of botany, zoology, and medicine, among others. In all these ways and more, the investigation of biochemical reactions of living organisms continues to be vital in expanding upon existing knowledge of life-forms.

GLOSSARY

adenosine triphosphate (ATP) A molecule that stores and then releases chemical energy from food molecules. ATP is found in the cells of all living things.

amino acid Any of 20 different kinds of tiny, basic molecules that link into long chains to form proteins. Amino acids are called the "building blocks" of proteins.

carbohydrate An organic substance formed by green plants during the process of photosynthesis that serves as an important food source for animals. Carbohydrates are also part of the structure of the nucleic acids of all living things.

carbon A relatively uncommon chemical element that is essential for life on Earth.

catalyst A substance, such as an enzyme, that changes the rate of a chemical reaction without being changed itself.

centrifugal Moving, proceeding, or acting in a direction away from a center or axis.

chain reaction A self-sustaining sequence in which products yield new products that initiate further processes of the same kind.

chloroplast A structure within a plant cell in which light energy is absorbed and converted to chemical energy, a process called photosynthesis.

energy The capacity for something to do work.

entropy A measure of how much of the energy generated by a process can be used for work.

enzyme A protein that works as a catalyst by changing the rate of chemical reactions in living organisms.

glucose A carbohydrate, or simple sugar, that is found in fruits, honey, and in the cells of many animals, where it helps to regulate cell metabolism.

hormone A substance secreted by both animals and plants that help to regulate the physical processes of the organism.

hydrolysis A double decomposition reaction with water as one of the reactants.

light Electromagnetic radiation that can be detected by the human eye. It is made up of waves of particles known as photons.

lipid An organic substance, such as a fat or oil, that resists interaction with water.

metabolism The process by which food is converted into energy through complex chemical reactions in the cells of living organisms.

mitochondrion An organelle contained in the cytoplasm of most eukaryotic cells that produces energy (adenosine triphosphate) for the cell.

pepsin An enzyme in the gastric juices of the stomach that allows animals to digest foods with protein.

peptide A compound that is made up of chains of amino acids, similar to proteins but smaller.

photosynthesis The process by which autotrophs such as green plants transform light energy into food.

polymer A compound made up of large connected molecules, which are composed of small molecules called monomers.

protein A compound made up of amino acids that are arranged in a complex structure.

stoichiometry The study of the proportions at which different chemical entities, such as elements and compounds, react with each other.

stomate A tiny opening in the skin of a leaf that allows carbon dioxide in and water vapour out.

telomere Repeating segment of DNA that appears at the ends of chromosomes in eukaryotic cells. Because some segments are lost every time a cell is replicated, the number of repeats determines how long a cell will live.

thermodynamics The way that heat and cold relate to energy.

BIBLIOGRAPHY

BIOCHEMISTRY

Overviews of biochemical reactions are David L. Nelson and Michael M. Cox, *Lehninger Principles of Biochemistry*, 7th ed. (2017); and Jeremy M. Berg, Lubert Stryer, and John L. Tymoczko, *Biochemistry*, 8th ed. (2015).

Particular topics are addressed in J. Etienne-Decant and F. Millot, *Genetic Biochemistry: From Gene to Protein* (1988; originally published in French, 1987), an overview of information flow from genes to proteins; Maria C. Lindner (ed.), *Nutritional Biochemistry and Metabolism: With Clinical Applications*, 2nd ed. (1991), on the dynamic roles that nutrients play in the structure and function of the human body; and P.K. Stumpf and E.E. Conn (eds.), *The Biochemistry of Plants: A Comprehensive Treatise* (1980–).

CHEMICAL REACTIONS

John C. Kotz, Paul M. Treichel, and John R. Townsend, *Chemistry & Chemical Reactivity*, 9th ed. (2015), intended for university students, contains examples of chemical reactions woven into descriptions of chemical principles. William H. Brown, Christopher S. Foote, Brent L. Iverson, and Eric Anslyn, *Organic Chemistry*, 7th ed. (2014), describes the principles of organic chemistry, with chemical reactions organized by the type of molecule undergoing reaction and by the type of reaction. N.N. Greenwood and Alan Earnshaw, *Chemistry of the Elements*, 2nd ed. (1997), is an advanced textbook and reference book for inorganic chemistry that presents a broad overview of chemical reactions, organized by element.

METABOLISM

Comprehensive information on metabolism is provided in James Darnell, Harvey Lodish, and David Baltimore, *Molecular Cell Biology*, 5th ed. (2004); T.A.V. Subramanian (ed.), *Cell Metabolism, Growth and Environment*, 2 vol. (1986); David A. Bender, *Amino Acid Metabolism*, 3rd ed. (2012); and Valdur Saks (ed.), *Molecular System Bioenergetics: Energy for Life* (2007).

PHOTOSYNTHESIS

Photosynthesis is discussed in David W. Lawlor, *Photosynthesis*, 3rd ed. (2001); Hans Lambers, F. Stuart Chapin III, and Thijs L. Pons (eds.), *Plant Physiological Ecology*, 2nd ed. (2008); and Lincoln Taiz and Eduardo Zeiger (eds.), *Plant Physiology*, 6th ed. (2014). Technical treatments that consider the biochemistry of photosynthesis include Robert E. Blankenship, *Molecular Mechanisms of Photosynthesis*, 2nd ed. (2008); and Philip Stewart and Sabine Globig (eds.), *Photosynthesis: Genetic, Environmental and Evolutionary Aspects* (2011). Photosynthesis in algae and other aquatic plants is considered in Paul G. Falkowski and John A. Raven, *Aquatic Photosynthesis*, 2nd ed. (2007); and John T.O. Kirk, *Light and Photosynthesis in Aquatic Ecosystems*, 3rd ed. (2011).

INDEX

INDEX

DNA, 17, 22–23, 66–67, 172, 203, 208–209, 220, 224, 232–234, 237, 249, 286

E

electrophoresis, 60–61
elimination reactions, 51–52
Embden, Gustav Georg, 101
Emerson, Robert, 268
endothermic reactions, 33, 34, 58
entropy, 34–35, 68, 160, 161, 162
exothermic reactions, 33, 35

F

Fischer, Emil, 20
fluorescence, 264
free energy, explanation of, 160

G

gas-forming reactions, 38–39
glucose catabolism, 95–99
  aldolase reaction, 100
  formation of ATP, 100–108
  phosphogluconate pathway, 108–113
glucose metabolism, research on, 185–187

H

Hill, Archibald V., 102–103
Hill, Robert, 253–254, 265
hormones, 17, 28–29, 185, 187, 231, 310
Houssay, Bernardo Alberto, 185–186
hydrolysis reactions, 55–56
hydrothermal vents, 42–43

I

Ingenhousz, Jan, 11, 238
intermediary metabolism, 19, 64
isomerization, 151
isotopes, use of in studying metabolism, 16, 63

K

Kendrew, John Cowdery, 20–21
Krebs, Hans, 76, 77–78, 91
Krebs cycle/TCA cycle
  ATP yield of aerobic oxidation, 153–154
  formation of coenzyme A, carbon dioxide, and reducing equivalent, 145–150
  regeneration of oxaloacetate, 151–153